O Riker

OUR LADY OF LIGHT

OUR
LADY
OF
LIGHT

TRANSLATED AND ABRIDGED

FROM THE FRENCH

OF

CHANOINE C. BARTHAS

AND

PÈRE G. DA FONSECA, S.J.

THE BRUCE PUBLISHING COMPANY
MILWAUKEE

Nihil obstat: JOHN A. SCHULIEN, S.T.D., Censor librorum
Imprimatur: ✠ MOYSES E. KILEY, Archiepiscopus Milwaukiensis
January 30, 1947

PREFACE BY THE GENERAL EDITOR

Among the momentous events of our twentieth century we cannot fail to mention, as of utmost interest and significance, the luminous apparitions of our Lady to three shepherd children in a mountainous recess of Portugal: Jacinta, Francis, and Lucy, the three little seers who will enter into our lives never to be forgotten.

On predicted days, at the place assigned, in the presence of ever increasing multitudes, the heavenly visits took place, culminating finally in the overwhelming spectacle of light enacted in a noonday sky on the last day of the apparitions. It was God's own fiery signature, as has been well remarked, that now flamed across the heavens in the sight of some sixty thousand witnesses, confirming all that here had been said and done by Mary Immaculate.

But of greatest importance to us is her message itself as conveyed in these pages.

The basis of the present volume is the authoritative work issued by the Portuguese Jesuit, Gonzaga da Fonseca, professor at the Biblical Institute at Rome, and adapted in a French translation by Canon Barthas. The latter book has met with high commendations and won the special approbation of the Holy See. It has been used to best advantage in the English rendition offered here, suited in particular to our English-reading public and retaining all the full reliability of the original.

JOSEPH HUSSLEIN, S.J., PH.D.
General Editor, Science and Culture Series

St. Louis University
January 14, 1947

CONTENTS

PART IV: MIRACLES

PART V: DOCUMENTARY PART

OUR LADY OF LIGHT

1

PORTUGAL AND FÀTIMA

"MARY'S LAND"

As early as the seventh century, the old Roman province of Lusitania was conquered by the Saracens or Moors. Toward the end of the eleventh century, Alphonsus VI, King of Leon and Castile, reconquered part of it. In the beginning of the twelfth century, Alfonso Henriquès won a great battle over the Moors, at Ourique, and his enthusiastic soldiers at once proclaimed him king.

His suzerain, Alphonsus of Castile, protested against this usurpation, but Henriquès asked for and obtained the protection of the pope. So Portugal was born — and born Catholic. The Portuguese nation has never forgotten this papal origin, and through the centuries has remained Catholic at heart, despite freemasonry, revolution, the loss of its monarchy, and, in 1910, the proclamation of the republic. A sad period of disorder, anarchy, and religious persecution seemed to portend the total loss of that country which still called itself "Mary's Land."

Its daughters and even its sons had loved to bear our Lady's name or that of her feasts: Maria da Conceiçâo, da Purificaçâo, da Assunçâo, das Dores (Dolors), do Carmo (Carmel), etc. Its peasants and workmen had built chapels, churches, and oratories on all the hills and at all the crossroads in her honor. Nearly all the corporations and guilds had taken her for their heavenly protectress.

Even in the midst of the triumph of unbelief, some thirty years ago, the holy custom of the daily rosary had been maintained in many country families.

1

This was especially true of the region surrounding the celebrated Dominican monastery of Our Lady of Victory de Batalha (the Battle) which commemorated the thrilling times when Portugal was struggling to become a Christian nation.

This region, which is the geographical center of the country, is also, in a certain sense, its historical center. And, since Mary has accomplished here the "wonderful prodigies" about to be related, it has become its spiritual and mystical center as well.

FÀTIMA

By 1917, World War I had been raging for three years. Pius X had died of sorrow. Benedict XV had tried in vain to stop the conflagration. The little Portuguese nation had entered the conflict a year before. Now it saw the flower of its youth and its poor resources sinking into the abyss of war. On all sides, ruin, desolation, death.

The sovereign pontiff called upon all the Catholics of the world to organize a crusade of prayer *to obtain the peace of the world through the intercession of Mary*. At the same time he commanded that the invocation, "Queen of Peace, pray for us," be added to the litany. That letter was dated May 5, 1917. Eight days later, on Sunday, May 13, Our Lady of the Rosary showed herself to three little shepherds in the land of Portugal. She appeared to them again five times, insistently recommending the recitation of the rosary *"to ask for the end of the war,"* for *"only Mary can obtain this grace for men."* The voice of heaven echoed the voice of the vicar of Christ.

Soon, from one end of Portugal to the other, one word was heard over the sounds of battle, like the far-flung clarion call of peace: "Fàtima! Fàtima!"*

What idea did these syllables with their oriental sounds evoke?

In history and geography that name recalled only the daughter of Mahomet, who died in 632, leaving her name, in the tenth century, to the Fatimite dynasty. Nevertheless, the name Fàtima is now known not only to Portugal but throughout all Europe and

---

* The first *a* of Fàtima is strongly accented in pronunciation.

America, and even to the farthest parts of the world. It is everywhere blessed and celebrated with ever increasing enthusiasm.

Fàtima is a little parish about seventy miles north of Lisbon, in
the district of Santarem. It contains about forty hamlets lost in the
recesses of a mountain, the Serra de Aire, with a population of
about two thousand five hundred. The Arabian name of this locality
proves its antiquity and recalls a doubtful though oft-related legend.

In 1158, when half of Portugal was still under the Mohammedan
yoke, a brilliant cavalcade of Moorish youth of both sexes left the
castle of Alcacer do Sal, in the early morning, going toward the
River Sado for a day's rejoicing. But they marched straight into
a Portuguese ambuscade under the command of the fearless leader,
Gonçalo Herminguès. Most of the Moorish cavaliers fell bravely
in the fight, and the ladies of the escort were brought to Santarem
to be presented to the king, don Alfonso Henriquès, then warring
against the Saracens.

The king praised the bravery of his knights and asked their
leader what reward he desired.

"The honor of having served you, Sire," was his reply, "and in
memory of this day I would beg for the hand of Fàtima."

That was the name of the noblest and most beautiful of the
captives, the daughter of the *vali* or governor general of Alcacer.

"Good!" answered the monarch, "on condition that the young
princess freely accepts our holy faith and consents to be your wife."

Fàtima accepted. She received instruction and was baptized
under the name of Ouréana. The marriage was celebrated, and the
king gave Don Gonçalo, as a wedding gift, the city of Abdegas,
henceforth called Ouréana (the modern Ourém).

The beautiful princess died in the flower of youth. Broken-
hearted, Gonçalo gave himself to God in the Cistercian Abbey
of Alcobaço, and from that abbey, a few years later, a monastery
was founded in a neighboring mountain village. Father Gonçalo
was named superior. As soon as the chapel was built, he had the
remains of Ouréana buried there, where they may still remain,
though unmarked. But the place bears her name: Fàtima. The
chapel, with the changes of centuries, is the actual parish church.

A PEACEFUL HAMLET

The development of the Sanctuary of the Cova da Iria has changed the aspect of the whole country. Before that, to connect the plateau of Fàtima with the towns in the plain, there were only irregular paths and neglected roads.

Standing in one of these narrow, deeply hollowed roads, the tourist would perceive nothing but stones and rocky masses. Generations, one after the other, have piled up the stones from their fields along the roads and between their properties. These heaps form broad walls, often used as roadways. In the space between, splendid harvests of wheat and Indian corn are produced. Among the stones, here and there, grow sturdy vines which furnish the small quantity of wine required by the mountaineers.

In such a landscape, a few minutes from the straggling village of Fàtima, stand ten or twelve low, small houses set along the narrow, rocky road but separated by farmyards and gardens. It is the hamlet of Aljustrel.

The inhabitants are rough, hard-working mountaineers. Their monotonous life, busy with the slow, persistent cultivation of that originally ungrateful soil, is varied only by the Sunday Mass and by rarer descents to the fairs at Vila Nova de Ourém.

The little, one-story cottages are tiled and whitewashed; they have two small windows and a narrow door, reached from the road by two or three stone steps. Within, the same rustic, and to modern minds somewhat insufficient, furniture is everywhere to be seen. On the walls, however, is the crucifix, and many holy pictures bespeak the piety of the inhabitants.

Beside the house are the sheepfold and the outhouses. Behind are the farmyard and the garden where, amid other beautiful fruit trees, the fig tree is most abundant. In the shadiest corner is the "well." There are no springs in that country, so the well is only a cistern dug out of the rocks, collecting rain water which, however, remains fresh throughout the summer.

At the time our story opens, two of these houses belonged to two brothers-in-law, Antonio dos Santos and Manuel Pedro Marto; the first in the lower part of the hamlet, the other on the heights.

Manuel Pedro's house was comparatively new. It had been built for the first marriage of his wife, Olimpia, who, when he married her, was a widow with two children. Nine other sons and daughters came to people that house. Francisco (Francis), born on June 11, 1908, and Jacinta, born on March 10, 1911, were the youngest of this numerous family.

Manuel Pedro's sister, Maria Rosa, was married to Antonio dos Santos, a good, honest workman, but less zealous than his brother-in-law about his own business. In his house lived a son and four daughters, of whom the youngest had received the name of Lúcia de Jésus (Lucy of Jesus) in baptism. She came into the world on March 22, 1907. One of Antonio's daughters was married and his only son was in the army. Olimpia's two younger ones and Maria Rosa's youngest daughter were to have the most wonderful adventure that may well befall Christian children.

At the time of the great apparitions granted them by Mary, Lucy, the eldest, was scarcely ten years old, Francis was nine, and his sister, Jacinta, was just seven. They had been occupied for a few months with keeping the sheep of their respective families. Lately, however, they had put the two flocks together and brought them to pasture in partnership. Who could have suspected that these three little shepherds, untutored and ignored, had been chosen by the Queen of Heaven to be the heroes of the greatest supernatural and mystical drama of our troubled times?

2

APPARITIONS OF THE ANGEL
(1916)

WONDERFUL STORIES

Lucy, Francis, and Jacinta were already hiding a great secret, which the two younger children were to keep until their early death, and which ecclesiastical authority has only lately revealed (May, 1942). An angel had appeared to them and spoken to them several times, apparently to prepare the future confidants of our Lady for their special mission.

These events were authenticated both in Portugal and in Rome. His Eminence, Cardinal Cerejeira, Patriarch of Lisbon, at the Pontifical Mass at the Cova da Iria on May 13, 1942, solemnly affirmed their truth before hundreds of thousands of people.

Almost at the same time, the fourth Italian edition of *Le Meraviglie di Fàtima* by Father da Fonseca appeared in Rome revealing the wonderful events about to be related. This Vatican polyglot edition bore the *imprimatur* of the Holy Father's vicar general.

Before leading out their flocks, Lucy, Francis, and Jacinta were accustomed to say an Our Father and a Hail Mary in honor of their guardian angels. Not in the least ungrateful, these holy spirits must in turn have invisibly accompanied them in their day's work. When, later, Sister Lucy was begged by the bishop to relate all she could tell of the events of their childhood, she affirmed that an angel had appeared to them many times and that he had familiarly taught them to prepare themselves for the "merciful designs" of the Lord upon them.

Here is the account she gives of the three principal visits of the heavenly spirit.

"PRAY LIKE THAT!"

It was about the time when Francis and Jacinta had obtained their parents' permission to keep their flock with Lucy's, toward the end of the spring of 1916. Lucy, the eldest, could not assign the exact date, "because," as she later explained, "I did not know as yet how to keep count of the years, nor the months, nor even the days of the week." The three children had led their sheep into a property belonging to the Santos, below the Cabeço hill, called the Old Garden.

A very fine drizzling rain fell about the middle of the morning, and so the little group, followed by their sheep, climbed up the hillside looking for some rock that might protect them.

"Thus," says Sister Lucy, "we entered that blessed grotto for the first time."

This cavity in the rocks was halfway up the hill, on land belonging to Lucy's godfather. Here trees and thick shrubbery effectively hid the oft-mentioned "Cabeço Grotto."

The rain stopped before long and the bright sun reappeared in the dazzling blue sky; but the little shepherds remained in their shelter until about noon, when they ate their frugal meal, said their beads, and then played jackstones with small pebbles.

Suddenly a gust of wind startled them. Instinctively they turned about toward the plain, for around them everything was calm.

Above the olive trees that covered the slope below them they saw a dazzling light, and in the midst of it, coming toward them, a human form. It was white, whiter than snow, and seemed like a crystal statue radiant throughout with sunlight. As it drew nearer, they could make it out to be a youth of fourteen or fifteen, superhumanly beautiful.

Coming upward toward the children, he said sweetly: "Do not be afraid, I am the Angel of Peace. Pray with me."

With that he went down on his knees, and bowing his forehead to the ground, repeated three times: "My God, I believe, I adore,

I hope, and I love Thee! I beg pardon for those who do not believe, nor adore, nor hope, nor love Thee."

Yielding to a supernatural impulse, the three children had prostrated themselves like him, and now repeated the words they had heard him say. Then the angel rose, adding: "Pray like that. The Most Holy Hearts of Jesus and Mary will be touched by your prayers."

The mysterious figure disappeared.

Twenty-five years later, Sister Lucy thus recalled her impressions:

"The supernatural atmosphere enveloping us was so intense that, for a long while, we scarcely realized our own existence, remaining as the angel had left us, ever repeating the same prayer.

"The presence of God was felt so intensely, so intimately, that we could not speak even to one another. The next day our souls were still wrapt in that atmosphere which disappeared only little by little.

"No one spoke about this apparition, nor thought of recommending secrecy to the others. It was not easy to speak of so intimate a grace. Perhaps, too, because it was the first one, it made so strong an impression upon us."

So deeply were the words of the angel impressed upon the minds of the children that they never forgot them. Henceforth, when left unnoticed, they would prostrate themselves as they had seen the angel do and repeat the prayer the angel had taught them, till they could no longer pronounce the words or keep that painful position.

Lucy, Francis, and Jacinta kept the most absolute silence about this mysterious visit, speaking about it only among themselves. The little, solitary Cabeço grotto, where their mystical vocation had begun, became very dear to them and was later their favorite place of meditation and penance.

"FOR THE CONVERSION OF SINNERS"

Two months later, during the intense heat of summer, which here extended from July to the middle of August, when the older people were taking their midday siesta, our three little friends happened to be in Lucy's garden. This was situated "behind the well," another favorite spot because of the quiet solitude found there.

Suddenly, without any previous warning, the mysterious Cabeço visitor was again beside them.

"What are you doing here?" he said. "Pray, pray much! The Holy Hearts of Jesus and Mary have plans of mercy in regard to you. . . . Continually offer up prayers and sacrifices to the Lord."

At this point Lucy asked a question: "How shall we make sacrifices?"

"You can make sacrifices of all things," came the reply. "Offer them in reparation for all the sins that offend God, and beg of Him the conversion of sinners. In this way, try to draw down peace upon your country. I am its guardian angel, the Angel of Portugal. Above all, accept and bear humbly the sufferings the Lord will wish to send you."

These words penetrated the children's minds "like a light, which gave them to understand how much God loved them and how much He wished to be loved; how great, too, the value of sacrifice, and how much the Lord takes it into account for the conversion of sinners." From that moment, Lucy, Francis, and Jacinta set themselves to offer to the Lord all that they could suffer for His sake. But their favorite penance was to remain, hour after hour, prostrate upon the ground, repeating the prayer the angel had taught them in his first apparition.

THE MYSTIC COMMUNION

It was the end of September or the beginning of October. After taking their slight meal in a field belonging to the Santos at the foot of the Cabeço hill, the little shepherds went up to the grotto to say their beads and the angel's prayer. They had repeated that formula many times over, when they suddenly found themselves surrounded by a wonderful brightness.

They rose then and saw the angel beside them. This time he held a chalice, above which was a host. From that white host drops of blood were flowing.

Leaving the chalice, which remained mysteriously suspended in the air, he knelt beside the children and made them repeat the following words three times:

"Most Holy Trinity, Father, Son, and Holy Spirit, I adore You profoundly, and offer You the Most Precious Body, Blood, Soul, and Divinity of our Lord Jesus Christ, present in all the tabernacles of the world, to repair the outrages by which He is Himself offended.

"By the infinite merits of His Sacred Heart and by the intercession of the Immaculate Heart of Mary, I beg for the conversion of all poor sinners."

The angel rose, took the host, and presented it to Lucy who received it. Then he divided the chalice between Jacinta and Francis, saying at the same time:

"Take the Body and the Blood of Jesus Christ, horribly outraged by ungrateful men. Repair their sins and console your God!"

Then, prostrating himself, he said the prayer, three times again: "Most Holy Trinity . . ." and disappeared.

The children remained on their knees in the same position, repeating the same prayer, unable to tear their thoughts from the heavenly vision, nor from the mysterious Communion they had just received. The presence of God totally absorbed them, depriving them even of their bodily senses.

Francis was the first to recover and recall the others to the realities of earth. Evening was falling: it was time to go home.

This time, too — in fact, this time especially — they said nothing about the heavenly visit.

3

THE FIRST VISIT OF THE "LADY"
(May 13, 1917)

A MAY MORNING

On this beautiful Sunday morning, May 13, 1917, having been to Mass, Lucy, Jacinta, and Francis had brought their flocks together. Before leaving, they had not failed to say the Our Father and the Hail Mary in honor of their guardian angels.

Leaving the hamlet at a place called the Claypit, they stopped to discuss where they would lead the sheep. By chance, or rather by the guidance of divine providence and the inspiration of the Blessed Virgin, they chose from among eight or ten possible places the one called the Cova da Iria.

This place is now so famous that the terms must be explained. *Cova* means a hole, a cavity, a bucket. The allusion here is to the fact that the land assumes the shape of a natural amphitheater, over five hundred yards in diameter. *Iria* is very probably the name of St. Iria or Irene, who dwelt in this region in the seventh century. Her feast is on the twentieth of October. She gave her name to the town of Santarem, i.e., Santa Irena.

To get to the Cova, the little shepherds had to retrace their steps and walk about a mile and a half along a winding path that has now disappeared because of improvements in local roads. Lucy's parents owned a partly sterile piece of land at the Cova, which produced mainly holly oaks and a few olive trees. The children had driven in their sheep at about midday, and the hour for breakfast was drawing near. They were not anxious now about their flocks, for the nice fresh grass would provide a good meal for them. They, therefore, proceeded to take their own. Then Lucy suggested

11

that they should say their beads. How could they fail to say them in this month consecrated to Mary? Besides, the angel had urged them to pray with fervor. They knelt down on the grass, in the shade of an olive tree.

This duty fulfilled, they drove their sheep up the slope toward the top of the hill. There, without losing sight of their flock, they could play a favorite game, building a house. Lucy and Jacinta brought the materials, Francis did the building. Soon, a little stone circle rose up, filled with a heap of pine needles.

It was a prophetic symbol, though the young masons hardly guessed it. That little project stood on the very spot where, in a few years, was to rise the great basilica of Our Lady of Fàtima, the largest church in Portugal.

THE BEAUTIFUL VISITOR

It was high noon. The sun was at its zenith. Suddenly a kind of vivid lightning dazzled the little shepherds. Alarmed, they searched the sky. Not a cloud!

Lucy had heard of sudden storms in May. There might be one gathering behind the mountains. "Let's go home! The storm may catch us here!"

No less frightened than she, her cousins agreed; so they gathered their sheep together and drove them down the hill, toward the right.

When they had reached the foot of the declivity, where the miraculous stream now flows, another flash, more dazzling than the first, held them riveted to the spot. Silenced by fear, they anxiously glanced at one another, then continued to follow their sheep.

A few steps farther, three or four yards from a little holm tree, they found themselves surrounded by a light so strong that it almost blinded them. Obeying one same impulse, all three looked to the right. Before them, above the little holm, in the center of that halo surrounding them also, they saw a beautiful lady, brighter than the sun. Terrified, they sought to flee. But a maternal gesture and a sweet word held them back.

"Do not be afraid. I will do you no harm!"
Then the children, falling into an ecstasy, contemplated her.

The wonderful "young lady," as they first spoke of her, seems to them now to be eighteen at the most. She resembles no picture of the Blessed Virgin or of the saints that they have ever seen.

Her dress, white as snow, falls to her feet. It is fastened about her neck by a golden cord that comes down to her waist.

A veil (or "mantle"), white too, with edges decorated in fine gold embroidery, covers her head and shoulders, and then falls almost to the hem of her dress, enveloping her whole body.

The face, pure, infinitely delicate, beams in the sun's rays, smiling lovingly, with a touch of sadness.

The hands are joined at the breast. From the right arm hangs a string of beads of pearly whiteness, finished with a cross of burnished silver.

The feet, bare and rosy, rest lightly on an ermine cloud that just touches the green branches of the shrub.

After twenty-five years, Sister Lucy had not forgotten the slightest trait of this heavenly vision. But when asked to describe it, she could use but one word: *light*.

Five years ago, writing about a picture of Our Lady of Fàtima with which she was not at all satisfied, she made the following remarks to the bishop of Leiria:

"It seems to me, that if I could paint — without being able to paint her as she is, which is impossible since one cannot even describe her with words of this earth — I would clothe her with a dress as simple and white as possible, and a 'mantle' falling from the top of the head to the edge of the robe. And since I could not paint the light and beauty that adorned her, I would suppress all, except a fine gold fillet on the edge of the mantle. This ornament shone on the background of light, like a ray of the sun, shining more intensely than the rest. This comparison is far, indeed, from the truth, but I cannot express it better."

FIRST CONVERSATION

The "lady" looked at the children, and Lucy made bold to ask: "Where do you come from, Madam?"

"*I come from heaven.*"

"And what are you coming here for?"

"*I come to ask you to meet here six times in succession, at this same hour, on the thirteenth of each month. In October, I will tell you who I am and what I expect of you.*"

After a few moments of silence, Lucy asked again:

"You come from heaven. . . . And I, shall I go to heaven?"

"*Yes, you will come.*"

"And Jacinta?"

"*She, too.*"

"And Francis?"

The eyes of the apparition turned then more directly upon the little boy, with an expression of kindness and maternal compassion.

"*He, too. But first, he must say his beads very often.*"

The conversation continued between the shepherds in ecstasy and the mysterious "young lady." The children could never forget a single word of it, but no one else would ever know all its words because the "seers," by common agreement, would never reveal what seemed to them indiscretion or vanity to report.

They have said, however, that the lady reassured them about the eternal lot of two young girls who had recently died in the parish. One was already in heaven, the other in purgatory.

About three years ago, in a copybook written for the bishop of Leiria, Sister Lucy revealed a hidden detail which, in a remarkable manner, now that it is known, reveals the penitent life of the little seers of Fàtima and explains its true meaning.

"*Will you,*" the lady asked the children, even at that first appearance, "*offer sacrifices to God and accept all the sufferings He will send you in reparation for the numberless sins which offend His divine Majesty? Will you suffer to obtain the conversion of sinners, to repair blasphemies, as well as all the offenses committed against the Immaculate Heart of Mary?*"

"Yes, we will!" Lucy answered with enthusiasm, in the name of all three.

By a gesture of maternal kindness, the vision showed how this childlike enthusiasm pleased her. Then, she added: *"You will, therefore, have much to suffer, but the grace of God will assist you, and always bear you up."*

Saying these words, the apparition separated her hands which till then she had held joined together, and this simple gesture caused a mysterious ray of light, intense and intimate, to flow toward the seers, "penetrating to the depths of their souls [Sister Lucy's own words], and causing them to see themselves in God more clearly than in a radiant mirror. . . ."

Then, yielding to an irresistible impulse, the three little seers fell on their knees, earnestly repeating: "O Most Blessed Trinity, I adore You! . . . My God, my God, I love You!"

After a few moments, the apparition urged the children to say their beads every day, with devotion, to obtain the peace of the world and the conversion of sinners.

Then the lady moved away toward the east. She did not seem to move her feet, but went "quite straight, all of a piece." Soon the wonderful vision had vanished in the light of the sun.

AFTER THE ECSTASY

Having recovered from their ecstasy, Lucy, Francis, and Jacinta joyfully looked at one another and exchanged their first impressions.

All three had seen the apparition perfectly, but Lucy alone had spoken to her. Francis had not even heard the voice of the beautiful lady, though he had heard all his cousin had said. Jacinta had heard everything distinctly, questions and answers, but she had taken no part in the conversation.

This circumstance alone proves the truth of the vision. Children inventing such an account would never have imagined this difference in their perceptions.

The dialogue between Lucy and the vision had lasted about ten minutes, almost time enough to say the beads right through.

And the flock? Francis was the first to notice that it had wandered away from its keepers. The greedy sheep had gone into a neighboring field of green vetch. The shepherds hastened to gather them in, much concerned about what had happened. They were going to have trouble, for that field belonged to another family! They found, however, on examining it, that no harm had been done. "Not a single piece of vetch had been eaten," as Lucy simply stated.

The three children cared no longer for play. Their hearts were content after this first meeting with heaven. In mute astonishment, they thought over what they had seen and heard.

Looking toward the east, they sought to catch a last glimpse of the halo surrounding the vanished virgin. Jacinta fervently joined her hands, as if to invoke the vision. But she could only say: "Wasn't that lady beautiful!"

Seeing her so enthusiastic, and feeling the consequences, Lucy said to her little cousin: "At least, don't tell everyone about it."

"I won't say anything! Nothing at all! Don't worry!"

Before the sun had set, they gathered their sheep together and drove them home. It was twilight when they reached Aljustrel. On saying good-by to her cousins at their sheepfold, Lucy warned them again: "Now be silent! You understand?"

"O yes," said Francis. "We won't tell."

A VILLAGE EVENT

They had supper at the Santos, and said night prayers. Antonio went out for a breath of fresh air. By the light of the oil lamp, Maria Rosa made one of her sons read a page of the Old Testament. Then they all went to bed.

It was not the same at the Martos. Jacinta could not bear the weight of her happiness. How could she hide it from her mother to whom she related the minutest events of each of her days?

Manuel Pedro and Olimpia had been absent all day. In the evening, Jacinta waited by the little road for her mother. It was already late when she saw her. Running up, she threw her arms around her neck — a thing she seldom did — and cried out:

"Mamma! Today, I saw the Blessed Virgin at the Cova da Iria!"

"Lord, what are you saying? Are you crazy?"

"It's true!"

"I don't believe it! You're not a saint to see the Blessed Virgin!"

"But it's true! Francis and Lucy saw her too!"

"You're a foolish little hussy!"

The child had become sad. "Believe me, Mamma!" And, when they were in the house, she said: "Mamma, Francis and I must say the beads. The Blessed Virgin told us to."

When they had finished their prayer, Jacinta came back to her mother. "Mamma," she said, "we must say the beads every day. The Blessed Virgin said so."

Then the father came in. The father, mother, eight children, a brother-in-law, and a nephew were at table there that evening. When they were all seated, Olimpia asked her daughter to tell them exactly what had happened.

The little girl told the whole family about the extraordinary event, minutely, with all the circumstances, and Francis confirmed everything she said; but, faithful to his promise, he added nothing and made no comment.

The next morning, as soon as she was up, Olimpia ran over to her sister-in-law to clear the thing up. But Maria Rosa knew nothing; her daughter had not spoken. She waited before speaking to her.

Meanwhile, Lucy had been warned by Francis that Jacinta had been indiscreet. The little cousin excused herself saying, with her hand on her heart: "There was something here that made me speak." Then she promised never to mention it again to anyone.

The silence between Lucy and her mother lasted a whole week. Then, one morning, when they were alone in the sheepfold, Maria Rosa questioned the child. Regretting that her cousin had failed to keep silence as agreed, Lucy told simply what she had seen.

Overcome by fear of what this story would draw upon them, Mrs. Santos easily persuaded herself that there were nothing but dreams and illusions in the whole affair. People were already making fun of it.

A few days later she spoke to the parish priest, Father Manuel Marquès Ferreira.

"Such misfortunes happen only to us!"

"What? You call it a misfortune?"

"Yes, that child is making us the laughingstock of the country."

"But, if what she says should be true, it would be a great blessing for you and everyone would envy you."

"Yes . . . if . . . but it can't be so. My daughter is lying. And it's the first time, too. But I'll teach her!"

When she got back to the house she did give her little girl the promised lesson with striking arguments.

The news spread rapidly, meeting unbelief everywhere, and tongues began to wag.

"Did you ever hear anything like it?"

"Such brats! They should be punished. It's the parents' fault!"

"They haven't enough sticks to keep them in order!"

To put a stop to it all, early one morning Maria Rosa called her little girl who was still in bed.

"Get up immediately! You are to go to the neighbors and tell them you have lied."

Lucy remained firm. Her mother coaxed her, threatened her, then took the broomstick and applied it vigorously. But she got only a respectful silence, and a confirmation of the whole story.

Finally, Maria Rosa let her go off to the pasturage, telling her to reflect all day.

"I have never accepted a lie from the mouths of my children. I am not going to accept any more deceit of that kind. This evening, I will take you around to every house in the hamlet. You will confess that you deceived them, and beg their pardon for it."

Lucy went to the mountain with her sheep and her sorrow. Francis and Jacinta were waiting for her, puzzled at her delay. Seeing her in tears, they asked why she was crying. She told them, and then added:

"My mother wants me to contradict everything I said. How can I?"

Immediately Francis blamed his sister. "You see, it's your fault. Why did you tell?"

Jacinta bent her head and cried. Then going down on her knees and joining her hands, she begged their pardon. "I have done wrong, but I promise never to speak about it to anyone."

That evening, when Lucy came home, her mother went back to her sermon on frankness, and concluded: "Listen! Now you are going to choose. Either you'll go and undeceive the neighbors, or else, I'll shut you up in a dark closet, where you'll not even see a bit of sunlight!"

Lucy's sisters repeated and exaggerated their mother's threats.

Poor little Lucy! How painful it all was for her! She would have wished to please her mother, but she saw no means of doing so. She could only break her heart by crying. They left her alone in a corner where she could cry to her heart's content, offering all the while her sacrifice to God, as the Lady had told her to do.

4

THE SECOND APPARITION
(June 13, 1917)

THE APPOINTMENT

The thirteenth of June was drawing near. Olimpia and her husband were willing to let their children keep their appointment with the Lady, but the Santos family was violently opposed to it.

However, in the surrounding villages even more than at Aljustrel, there were many people who wished to see this experience renewed. Some were even convinced of the truth of the apparition. Would it not be better to take these opinions into account?

Mrs. Santos herself was beginning to realize that the broomstick did not resolve the problem.

The day fixed by the Lady was the Feast of St. Anthony of Padua. This saint, most popular in Portugal, is called St. Anthony of Lisbon, because, although he died in Padua, he was born and lived twenty-five years of his short life in Lisbon, and is the patron saint of Portugal and of the parish of Fàtima.

The parents had counted much on this circumstance to keep their children at home and in the parish. But the little ones kept their resolution.

The evening before, Jacinta came to her mother and said:

"Mamma, don't go to the Feast of St. Anthony. Come with us to the Cova da Iria, to pray and see the Blessed Virgin."

"No, I won't go . . . nor you either. It's useless. The Blessed Virgin won't show herself."

"But, she will, Mamma! She said she would come back and she certainly will."

"Then, you don't want to go to the feast?"

"That Lady, Mamma, is so much more lovely! I'll go with Lucy and Francis to the Cova da Iria. If the Lady tells us we should go to the Feast of St. Anthony, then we'll go."

Early the next day, because they did not attach much importance to what the children said and doubtless because they thought their own affairs more important, Manuel Pedro and his wife left for the fair of Porto-de-Mos. They meant to purchase a pair of oxen and return in the evening.

The Santos, at the last moment, decided to remain neutral.

According to the custom on feast days, Lucy, Francis, and Jacinta led the flocks out very early and then brought them back. At about eleven, the little company of three could leave for their heavenly appointment. At noon they had spent a few minutes in saying their beads. How fervently, this time!

About sixty other people were there, perhaps more curious than convinced.

This is how one of these witnesses tells what he saw:

"The three children arrived at the appointed hour, and began the rosary, kneeling at the foot of a tall holm tree, about fifty yards from the place of the apparition. With the beads finished, Lucy rose, arranged her shawl, the kerchief over her head, and her dress, as she would have done before entering a church. Then she turned toward the east, waiting for the vision.

"We asked her whether we had long to wait and she said: 'No.' The two other children wanted to say their beads again. At that moment Lucy made a movement of surprise and said: 'There is the lightning! The Lady is coming!' And she ran down the slope toward the little holm tree of the apparition, followed by her cousins.

"I heard all that Lucy said to the vision, but I saw nothing and could not hear the answers. However, I noticed a remarkable thing: it was the month of June, and the tree had all its branches covered with long, fresh green shoots. Now, when Lucy announced that the Lady was moving away toward the east, all the twigs of the tree gathered together and bent toward that side, as if the Lady, when leaving, had let her dress drag over them."

HEAVENLY SECRETS

The vision and the conversation had lasted about ten minutes. For the children many feelings had been awakened during that short time.

Lucy again had begun the conversation: "What do you want of me, Madam?" The apparition once more told the children to come back the next month. She told them again to recite the beads every day, and she added: "*I want you to learn to read. Then, I will tell you what else I want.*"

Lucy asked for the cure of a sick person who had been recommended to her.

"*Let him be converted, and he will be cured within the year.*"

Then the Lady told each of the three children a secret, or rather, a first secret. Francis, who did not hear the Lady, was told by Lucy what concerned him.

It was conjectured that this "secret" concerned the children's future. It could not concern their eternal salvation, since in the first interview, the Lady had reassured them on that point. Doubtless, it was supposed, the Blessed Virgin had announced to the younger ones their approaching death, of which they seemed later to be so sure. She may also have advised Lucy to leave the world and embrace the religious life.

In fact, these suppositions are now known to have been correct. But there was another important detail. Sister Mary Lucia of Dolors (Lucy of Jesus) had received our Lord's permission to reveal part of the secret. This is what she wrote at the command of her confessor:

"On December 17, 1927, I asked our Lord in the Blessed Sacrament to let me know how I could satisfy the wish of my confessor that I should put down in writing certain graces received from God, if, in order to tell them, I would be obliged to speak of the secret confided to me by the Most Blessed Virgin.

"Jesus answered in a most distinct voice: 'My daughter, write all they ask you to. Write also what the Blessed Virgin revealed about . . . but, concerning the rest of the secret, keep silence as before.'"

The Three Seers of Fàtima: Jacinta, Francis, and Lucy

Manuel-Pedro Marto and Olimpia de Jésus — Parents of
Francis and Jacinta (1946)

General View of the Sanctuary

Cardinal-Patriarch and Crowd (May 13, 1942)
— The Silver Procession Banners

A View of the Basilica, Begun in 1928

The Tomb of Francis and Jacinta

Lucy had indeed asked the Blessed Virgin to bring her as well as her companions to heaven. In reply the vision answered:

"Yes, I will soon come to take Francis and Jacinta away. But you must remain longer here below. Jesus will use you to make me better known and more loved. He wishes to establish throughout the world the devotion to my Immaculate Heart."

"Then I shall remain alone?" asked Lucy, filled with grief at the thought of remaining without her confidants and friends.

"No, my child. You are suffering very much, but do not be discouraged. I will never forsake you. My Immaculate Heart will be your refuge and the way that will lead you to God."

This revelation regarding the future of the three children was, so to speak, wonderfully illustrated by what might be called a supplementary vision, the details of which have only recently been revealed.

As at the first appearance, so now again, the Blessed Virgin parted her hands while saying the above words, and a second time this gesture penetrated the hearts of the children with that same intense light in which they saw themselves as if plunged in God. It seemed to them that Francis and Jacinta were in one stream of light that rose up toward heaven, while Lucy was in another that diffused itself over the world.

Before the right hand of the apparition they could see a heart surrounded by thorns that pricked it on every side. The children understood that it was the Immaculate Heart of Mary, wounded by the sins of the world, and that it asked for penance and reparation.

Later they were convinced that the intense light that penetrated their breasts was intended to give them a more perfect knowledge and a more special love for the Immaculate Heart of Mary. From this day forth they felt in their hearts a more ardent love for the heart of their Mother in heaven.

To this account, Sister Lucy added: "That is what we had in mind when we said that the Lady had revealed a secret to us at the apparition in June. Truly, she did not tell us to be silent, but we felt that the Lord required it of us."

The vision disappeared, the children returned home, and the witnesses soon spread throughout the neighborhood all they heard from the mouth of the seers.

FIRST CONTRADICTIONS

The news of the heavenly visitations spread to the neighboring parishes. At Fàtima, they became the subject of every conversation. Some people, knowing the loyalty of the children, admitted the truth of the apparitions. But most were skeptical or hostile.

The priests of the neighborhood were nearly all incredulous, especially Father Marquès Ferreira, pastor of Fàtima.

Despite the second apparition, peace had not returned to the Santos house. On the contrary, the more the news spread, the more Maria Rosa sought to contradict her daughter.

The Martos, though convinced of their children's sincerity, feared that they were victims of some illusion. One day Olimpia said to them: "Be careful! Some day I'll punish you severely, because you deceive people!"

The children defended themselves. "We don't oblige people to go. Those who don't want to go, needn't go. But those who don't believe can expect to be punished by God."

At Jacinta's house they merely threatened the children. But Maria Rosa was violent. She scolded Lucy and even struck her for nothing, to such an extent that the pastor thought it his duty to warn her to be more moderate.

THE PASTOR'S INDECISION

It was a real joy for that mother to be invited by the pastor to bring her daughter to the priest's house to be questioned.

"My mother," wrote Sister Lucy, "was relieved, thinking that the pastor would take all the responsibility in the affair. She said to me: 'Tomorrow morning we are going to Mass. Then we'll go to see the pastor. Let him punish you. Let him do what he wants. Provided he makes you confess your lies, I'll be glad!'

"My sisters sided with my mother and threatened me with the worst sanctions, to frighten me."

Lucy went to tell her cousins what was going to happen. "We too," they said, "are going to the pastor's. He told Mamma to bring us. But he did not speak of punishment. Patience! If they beat us, we shall suffer it for the love of our Lord, and for poor sinners."

"The next morning, I went with my mother to the rector's. On the way she did not say a word. During Mass, I offered my sorrow to our Lord. As we were going up the steps to the priest's house, my mother said: 'Now, don't annoy me any more! You'll tell the pastor you lied so that next Sunday he may undeceive the people. After that it will be finished. What nonsense! To make people run all the way to the Cova da Iria to pray before a holly oak.'

"Then she knocked and opened the door.

"Contrary to all my mother's and my sisters' predictions, we were very kindly received by our priest, who quietly questioned me on all the events. Then he concluded, very calmly: 'It does not seem to me that all this comes from heaven. When our Lord communicates Himself to souls, He usually asks them to give an account of everything to their confessor or to their parish priest. This child, on the contrary, shuts herself up in silence. That may be a deceit of the devil. The future will reveal the truth.'"

The two younger children revealed nothing new to Father Ferreira. Francis answered all the questions simply and frankly. Jacinta put down her head and did not answer, or at most two or three words.

When they came out, Lucy asked why she was so silent, and she said: "You know I promised I would not talk to anyone."

Lucy was very well satisfied with the interview. The pastor had neither punished nor scolded her. He had not forbidden her to return to the Cova da Iria. He had only asked Maria Rosa to bring her little girl to see him after the events of the thirteenth of July.

Soon, however, one of the words spoken by the parish priest came back to her and worried her. He had said it might be a trick of the devil.

"How much that remark made me suffer only our Lord who reads hearts could say."

She often said to herself: "What if it is Satan who is trying to

get hold of my soul by that trick!" She had heard it said that the
spirit of evil always brings with him disorder and strife. Now,
since the day the "lady" had come, there had been neither joy nor
peace in their house.

She even reached the point of not seeing her cousins and of
hiding when they called for her. One day, however, she told them
of the fear that haunted her.

"That's not the devil," answered Jacinta. "No. It's not like him.
The devil is very ugly and he lives under the earth, in hell. That
lady is most beautiful. And we saw her going up to heaven."

This most logical reasoning cleared away her doubts. But she
confessed that, till the following apparition, her fervor and her
confidence diminished. Seeing her parents always against her, she
came to the point of asking herself whether it would not be better
to tell them she had lied, and be finished with it. But Francis and
Jacinta kept up her courage, saying: "Don't do that! You know
you would be telling a lie. And to tell a lie is to commit a sin."

All hesitation did not disappear, however. Lucy admitted that
for some time she was less fervent in her prayers and in making
sacrifices for sinners.

5

THE THIRD APPARITION
(July 13, 1917)

LUCY'S DISCOURAGEMENT

The number of believers was constantly increasing. In the neighboring hamlets many people believed in the truth of the apparitions and prayed fervently to the mysterious Lady, whose identity they guessed.

Among the first and the most enthusiastic must be named the two Carreiras, husband and wife. About this time (June–July) they determined to build a little rustic monument. It was a kind of arch, formed by two trunks of trees, roughly squared, and joined by a third trunk built horizontally. Above this was a cross, from which two lanterns were suspended and kept burning day and night.

They also built a little fence of rough stones, about three feet high, to protect the property about the holm tree. The little enclosure was completed by a rustic gate on the eastern side. Such was the first "sanctuary" of Fàtima.

However, the thirteenth of July was drawing near and Lucy was so discouraged that she had nearly given up the appointment with the Lady. She wrote thus, as Sister Mary Lucy:

"I was hesitating whether I would go to the Cova da Iria. I said to myself: 'If it is the devil, why should I go to see him? If they ask me why I don't go, I shall say I am afraid it is the devil we meet. Let Jacinta and Francis go if they want to. I shall not go any more to the Cova da Iria!'

"My resolution was made and I was determined to keep it.

"On the evening of the twelfth, a crowd of people began to arrive to witness the next day's events. Then I called my cousins and told them of my decision. They said: 'But we're going! That Lady told us to go!'

"Jacinta proposed to speak to the Lady in my place. But she regretted my not going, and began to cry. I asked her why.

" 'Because you are not going with us,' she said.

" 'No, I'm not going. If the Lady asks about me, tell her I have not come because I'm afraid it is a trick of the devil.'

"And I left them there to go and hide myself, so as not to answer the people who were looking for me.

"When I came back to the house that evening, my mother scolded me: 'There's our little girl! A little saint of rotten wood! All the time I leave her, after she has kept the sheep, she spends amusing herself so that we can't find her!'

"The next morning, as the time drew near when we ought to be setting out to meet the Lady, I felt myself drawn by some strange power which I could hardly resist. I set out, and stopped at my uncle's to see if Jacinta was still there. I found her with her brother Francis, kneeling at the foot of her bed, crying bitterly.

" 'Well,' I said, 'aren't you going? It is time.'

" 'Without you, we don't dare go. Come with us.'

" 'Well, I'm going.'

"Then their faces became radiant and they left with me."

Manuel Pedro and his wife accompanied the children. It seems that from this day they were both convinced, not only of the sincerity of their children, but even of the truth of the apparitions.

ANOTHER DIALOGUE

So many people were there this time, that the children had to push their way to get to the holm tree. It is believed that at least *four or five thousand people* were present — the first of the Fàtima crowds.

At exactly twelve, as on the preceding occasions, and in the same way, with a bright flash of lightning and in the midst of blinding light, the apparition was present to the children.

At Lucy's wish, the people went down on their knees. Doubtless deeply ashamed of her own hesitation and doubts, the child looked at the vision without daring to speak. It was Jacinta who broke out with: "Come, Lucy, speak! Don't you see that she is there already and that she wants you to speak to her?"

Then Lucy gathered courage to say again: "What do you wish me to do, Madam?"

The vision repeated with the same amiability what she had declared on the other occasions. Then she urged them to come on the thirteenth of the following month, and *insisted, for the third time, on their reciting daily the holy rosary in honor of the Blessed Virgin.*

"Say it with the intention of obtaining the end of the war. The intercession of the Blessed Virgin alone can obtain this grace for men."

Lucy expressed the desire to know the name of the heavenly visitor and asked her to give, by some miracle, a proof of the reality of her presence.

This request clearly shows the state of mind of the little seers, and even more, that of the crowd and of public opinion in general. A miracle would cause the doubts to vanish and the children would have nothing more to suffer. Poor innocents! The tempest was only beginning, and they scarcely imagined the cross awaiting them.

At Lourdes, Bernadette had asked the Blessed Virgin to make the rosebush flower at her feet, and our Lady had only smiled.

At the Cova da Iria Mary was more condescending, for, though she did not at once perform the miracle, she at least promised it.

"Continue to come every month. In October I will tell you who I am and what I desire."

Thus, having repeated her promise of the first apparition, she added: *"And I shall perform a great miracle so that the whole world may believe you."* (*Tout le monde*, "the whole world," may mean just that, or simply "everybody.")

Lucy continued: "I still have many things to ask you, Madam. Would you cure a poor cripple? . . . Convert a certain family at Fàtima? . . . Bring a certain sick person of Atougia to heaven as soon as possible?"

The vision answered that she would not cure the cripple any more than she would rid him of his poverty, but that he must recite the rosary every day with his family. The sick person must not lose patience; she knew better than he the best moment to come for him. As to the other persons, they would obtain the graces asked for in the course of the year, but they must recite the rosary.

Then, "to renew my cooled fervor," Sister Lucy humbly says, she again repeated: "*Sacrifice yourself for sinners, and say often, but especially when you are making some sacrifices: O Jesus, it is for love of You, for the conversion of sinners, and to repair the offenses offered to the Immaculate Heart of Mary.*"

During the apparition, the closer witnesses noticed a sad look on Lucy's face, and some heard a sigh, as of pain, escape her.

Finally, the little girl asked: "Is that all you wish me to do?"

"Yes," answered the Lady, "that is all." And the vision moved away as she had done before.

"Thank God," concluded Sister Lucy, telling of this vision, "this new interview with Mary cleared away all the shadows from my soul, and I found perfect peace."

After the departure of the Lady, the people crowded about the children, asking endless questions. Mr. Marto, fearing his little girl would be crushed, took her up in his arms, pushed his way through the crowd, and brought her home.

Lucy sought to satisfy the avid curiosity of the bystanders.

"Why are you so sad?"

"That is a secret."

"Good or bad?"

"It is for the good of us three."

"And for the people?"

"For some, it is good; for the others, it is bad."

Not one among the thousands of spectators had seen or heard the heavenly apparition. All, however, had been able to notice, for the first time, a pretty little cloud surrounding the children and covering the place of the apparition. All had also noticed a certain decrease in the light of the sun. These two phenomena ended at the very moment the vision disappeared.

THE SECOND AND PRINCIPAL SECRET PARTLY UNVEILED

To the account of the third apparition just given, a few more details can here be added that were disclosed at a later period.

Here is what Sister Lucy herself wrote before the twenty-fifth anniversary of the Fàtima apparitions. It was a statement made, she tells us, "out of pure obedience and with the permission of our Lord." Her text regards the "secret" just mentioned.

"The secret consisted of three distinct yet closely related things. I shall reveal two of them, the third must remain wrapped in mystery."

(The first of these concerns the vision of hell; the second, the prophecy of World War II.)

"When she said the last words quoted above ("Sacrifice yourself," etc.), our Lady once more stretched out her hands, as she had done twice before. The projected ray of light seemed to pierce the earth and we saw what looked like a great sea of fire. In this sea were plunged, black and burning, demons and souls in human form, resembling live transparent coals. Lifted up into the air by the flames, they fell back on all sides like sparks in a conflagration, with neither weight nor balance, amid loud screams and cries of pain and despair which made one tremble and shudder with terror.

"It was probably this sight that caused the exclamation of horror heard by the people.

"The devils were distinguished from the human beings by their horrible, disgusting, animal forms, unknown to us but transparent as live coals.

"This fearful sight lasted only a moment, and we must thank our heavenly Mother for having promised beforehand to take us to heaven, or I believe we should have died of horror and fear.

"Then, as if asking for help, we raised our eyes to the Blessed Virgin who said, kindly and sadly:

" 'You have seen hell, and the souls of poor sinners. To save them, our Lord wishes to establish in the world devotion to my Immaculate Heart. If people will do what I shall tell you [the reference here is evidently to the apparitions still to follow] many souls will be saved and there will be peace in the world!

" 'The war [that of 1914–1918] is coming to an end, but if the offenses against God do not cease, under the next pontificate [that of Pius XI] a still more terrible one will begin.' [There is question here, evidently, of the Civil War in Spain, which was in certain respects an international one and the prelude of World War II. The name of Pius XI is found, we believe, in Sister Lucy's manuscript.]

" 'To prevent that I shall come to ask the Consecration of the world to my Immaculate Heart and the Communion of Reparation on the First Saturday of the month.'

" 'If my requests are granted, Russia will be converted and there will be peace in the world [*l'on aura la paix*]. If they are not, Russia will spread its errors throughout the world, provoking wars and persecution against the Church; many good people will be martyred; the Holy Father will have much to suffer; many nations will be annihilated. [At this point ecclesiastical authority has imposed certain reticences.]

" 'But, finally, my Immaculate Heart will triumph.* [In what way? At the time willed, which will appear more clearly. In the meantime, however, we are given to understand that the] Consecration to the Immaculate Heart will take place [and that in consequence] Russia will be converted and a time of peace will be given to the world, etc.' "

The apparition concluded: "Tell this to no one, except Francis."

A few minutes after, she added: "When you recite the beads, after each decade say: *O my Jesus, forgive us our sins, save us from the fires of hell, and lead all souls to heaven, especially those that most need Thy mercy.*"**

---

* The Holy Father, Pius XII, consecrated the world to the Immaculate Heart, on October 31, 1942, in his message to the Portuguese people on the occasion of the Jubilee at Fàtima. He renewed this act on December 8, most solemnly, in St. Peter's Basilica.

** Those who first questioned the seers, believed that by the souls to be led into paradise were meant the souls in purgatory. However, there is question here, as everywhere else in the visions of Fàtima, of the salvation of *sinful souls*. The formula of this prayer that was circulated heretofore is erroneous.

What was the third still unknown detail of the "secret"? It will be revealed by Providence when the right moment comes. In any case, when one knows the horrors of the Spanish War (1936–1938) and those of World War II, it is not necessary to call attention to the agreement of events with the prophecy.

Let us notice, however, that the essential point of the secret is not the war, and that its aim is not to satisfy our curiosity, but to save souls eternally.

The secret affirms truly that man's greatest evil is sin, since it leads directly to hell, and that, on earth, it leads to wars and revolutions. It affirms also that temporal calamities are often the manifestations of divine justice provoked by the sins of man. The secret therefore calls us to repentance, without which the calamities of time would be only a prelude to eternal chastisement.

Finally, the secret recalls the Blessed Virgin's power to intervene and obtain the remedies of divine mercy for ourselves, for the Church, and for souls.

6

THE MASONIC SECT INTERVENES
THE FOURTH APPARITION
(August 19, 1917)

EXPECTATION

In the presence of Mary's beauty, Lucy had recovered peace of soul. Now she was sure that there would be a "sign of God" to prove the truth of the visions and that a miracle would overcome the opposition.

It was then, precisely, that the worst exterior trials began. The promise of a great miracle, repeated in every village, excited the curiosity of the Portuguese and multiplied the number of believers, sympathetic or admiring. But at Aljustrel and at Fàtima opposition still continued. Our Lord said truly: "No man is a prophet in his own country."

Lucy's mother slowly came around, but before her daughter she affected absolute disbelief. Yet she gave contributions for the lamps at the rustic arch, and her daughters helped to decorate the little altar put up for the thirteenth of August.

People came every day to pray before the evergreen oak, and relic lovers broke off its leaves and branches.

The fields of the Cova da Iria were trampled down. People complained and the mother blamed the children. "Those poor people come with confidence, deceived by your inventions. I don't know what to do to undeceive them!"

Father Ferreira, on his side, followed too blindly the instructions received from Lisbon, recommending prudence to all the clergy.

The Catholic press, not much developed at that time, observed a solemn reserve, advising its readers to beware of the possible machination of the powers of darkness.

On the other hand, the antireligious press, called "liberal," followed the events at Fàtima with excessive zeal. It told of interested people who wanted to open a miracle factory at Fàtima, a commercial exploitation of piety like at Lourdes. It set stories going that the seers had fits of epilepsy, that a mineral spring had been discovered, and that the vision would be a means of drawing people to profit by it, etc.

Not content with seeking to discredit the apparitions, the anticlerical politicians sought to "kill in the egg" this invasion of mysticism.

Fàtima depended politically upon the town of Vila-Nova de Ourém. The population there is extremely Catholic, but the administration, following the revolution of 1910, had fallen into the hands of a man who was practically the master and the terror of the neighborhood. He was surnamed the "Tinsmith" because of his profession, but his real name was Arthur d'Oliveira Santos.

As soon as he heard of the apparitions at the Cova da Iria, he set about carefully examining all the events. He soon decided to destroy this "reactionary" manifestation.

DECEPTION!

The articles in the masonic press had succeeded so far only in spreading the knowledge of Fàtima all through Portugal. Consequently, on the thirteenth of August, an immense crowd had gathered at the Cova da Iria.

"From every direction," wrote an eyewitness, "came innumerable crowds of people. Vehicles of every size and description endlessly followed one another. It is calculated that by noon at least eighteen thousand had assembled."

Most of them were devout pilgrims rather than curious sightseers. Crowded about the tree, now despoiled of all its leaves, they filled out the long wait by saying their beads and singing hymns.

At twelve o'clock, the seers had not yet appeared. Soon rumors spread that they would not come — they had been kidnaped by the Mayor of Ourèm!

There was an explosion of wrath among the people, who spoke of descending in a body to the town in order to call the impudent Tinsmith to account.

Happily for him, at this stage of the developments the attention of the crowd was drawn to another object.

Suddenly the thousands of people heard a tremendous clap of thunder which shook the clear skies, and they beheld a magnificent flash which sent streamers of light through the atmosphere. Everything happened exteriorly as if the children and the vision had been there. After the flash, which usually indicated that the Lady had come, a beautiful misty cloud formed near the green oak, remained there about ten minutes, and then rose into the air and dissolved itself. Everyone was satisfied, as if the Lady had really appeared.

By these prodigies, Mary showed that she, on her side, had not failed to keep the appointment.

The children, on the contrary, had failed, not through their fault but because the hour of trial had come for them. It is always so: God's great graces follow after great crosses, the unfailing mark of all heaven's works.

Not to delay here the account of the apparitions, the veritable martyrdom of the poor little seers during those cruel days (August 13–15, 1917) will be told in the third part of our narrative (page 101).

The crowd dispersed, feeling sure the vision would return only on the thirteenth of the next month. The children thought so too, and deplored their involuntary failure to meet the Lady at the appointed time. It was not to prove a failure, however.

THE APPARITION AT VALINHOS

Four days after their return from Vila-Nova, Lucy, Francis, and one of his other brothers, João (John), were keeping watch over their flocks at a place called Valinhos, between Aljustrel and the heights of Cabeço, when they saw the atmosphere take on the same tints it had at the Cova during the apparitions.

Surprised, they awaited the phenomenon and Lucy saw the flash of lightning, forerunner of the Lady's appearance. Then she begged John to run for Jacinta, who was at the house. As soon as the little girl arrived, the beautiful Lady showed herself.

At Valinhos there were evergreen oaks, just as at the Cova. It was on one of these trees, taller than at the Cova, that the Lady showed herself.

First she expressed sympathy for her little friends because they had been prevented from coming to the usual meeting place on the day appointed. Then she added that, *"because of the unbelief of the freethinkers, the miracle promised for October would be less striking."**

Afterward, she told them to go to the Cova da Iria on the two months following, at the date and the hour fixed.

Lucy, always practical, asked what was to be done with the offerings left by the faithful at the foot of the tree at the Cova. (There were over a hundred dollars which nobody wanted to touch.)

The Blessed Virgin answered that *it should be kept to solemnize the coming Feast of the Rosary.* For that day they should purchase two processional litters, one gold in color, the other silver. The first should be borne by Lucy and Jacinta, with two other little girls, the other by Francis and three of his companions, all dressed in white. The money remaining would help toward the building of a little chapel.

Lucy then asked for the cure of some sick people who had been recommended to her. The apparition said that she would cure some of them in the course of the year.

All this seemed secondary to the Blessed Virgin. She had not come for this. With a motherly tenderness, veiled with sadness, she *exhorted her little confidants to the practice of prayer and mortification.*

---

* That very day, at Fàtima itself, a Congress of Propaganda and Protestation against the "clerical lies" was held by the freethinkers.

She concluded: *"Pray, pray very much, and make sacrifices for sinners, for many souls go to hell because there is nobody to make sacrifices and to pray for them."*

Then the Lady disappeared. The vision had lasted the usual time.

As at the other times, the sight of the Lady was reserved to her three little friends. John had assisted, and his mother asked him that evening what he had seen.

"I saw Lucy, Francis, and Jacinta kneel down near the tree. Then I listened to what Lucy said. When she said: 'There, she is going! Look, Jacinta!' I heard a clap of thunder, like a rocket. But I saw nothing. Still, my eyes are sore from looking into the air." John, too, had seen the change in the sunlight.

Another interesting detail. The children, who complained of the people cutting away parts of the oak at the Cova, did not scruple to cut off the two branches on which the feet of the apparition had seemed to rest. Jacinta and Francis took them home.

Passing before the Santos house, they said to their aunt, who was standing with some people at the door: "Auntie, we saw the Blessed Virgin again!"

"You do nothing but see the Blessed Virgin, little liars that you are!"

"But we did see her. Look, Auntie! She had one foot on this branch and the other on that one."

"Liars! Let me see."

And Maria Rosa took the branches in her hand. Immediately all the people there smelled a delicious odor, of some unknown essence, exuding from the dark green foliage.

This phenomenon impressed Lucy's mother most strongly and, henceforth, she began to admit that her daughter might be telling the truth.

Antonio, too, began from that moment to defend Lucy when her mother or her sisters teased her too much.

"Do leave her alone! We don't know whether all she says is true, but we can't prove it to be false."

Now Lucy could live in something like peace at home. But

exterior difficulties were increasing — visits and interrogations were continual.

One day three policemen questioned the children lengthily, and finished with: "Reflect well, and decide to reveal that famous secret. Otherwise the mayor has decided to put you to death."

"Oh!" cried Jacinta, her face radiant, "I do love Jesus and the Blessed Virgin — that way we would much sooner go up to see them!"

The rumor continued to grow that they were seeking to kill the seers, and the idea spread of taking the children away from that part of the country, out of the power of the Tinsmith. But the children consulted together and refused to leave the hamlet, saying: "If they kill us, so much the better! We shall all the sooner go to heaven!"

7

THE SEPTEMBER VISIT

NEW ATMOSPHERIC PRODIGIES

The Portuguese were becoming more and more interested in the visions of the Cova da Iria.

The maneuvers of the administrator of the Counsel of Ourém had finally no other result than to demonstrate the sincerity of the seers. There were indignant protestations, and a considerable increase of faith in her who was already called Our Lady of Fàtima. The whole country waited with eager impatience for the thirteenth of September.

That morning, the roads leading to Fàtima were blocked with vehicles of every description and pedestrians of every class. One saw only true pilgrims, praying ardently.

At ten, the crowd had filled the sacred vale. The men came bareheaded. Soon nearly all were on their knees. Prayer, the beads, and sacred hymns arose on all sides. About noon the children arrived; then one could have counted from twenty-five to thirty thousand people. Yet it was in the middle of the grape harvest!

In her memoirs, Sister Lucy tells of their arrival on that day: "The roads were full of people who wished to speak to us. There was no human respect. Many people, pressing through the crowd, came to fall at our feet and beg us to present their petitions to our Lady. Others, unable to reach us, cried from afar, from the top of walls or from the trees on which they were perched to get a glimpse of us: 'For the love of God, ask the Blessed Virgin to cure my crippled son!' — 'May she cure my blind child!' — 'May she bring my husband back from the war!' — 'My son!' — 'Ask her to convert a sinner who is dear to me!' They thus recommended to us all the miseries of our poor humanity.

"And we, saying 'yes' to one, giving our hand to another that she might rise, kept on always advancing, helped by a few men who made a way for us through the crowd."

When they reached the place, Lucy asked the people to kneel down. Those who had still been standing now knelt, and an immense supplication, often mingled with tears, rose up to the Queen of Heaven.

At twelve o'clock exactly, the radiant sunlight began to lose its brightness and, as before, the atmosphere assumed a golden tint.

"What was felt during that rapid quarter of an hour can never be forgotten," says one witness, "but it is hard to describe. The sight of that immense crowd, the tense, anxious waiting, the fervor of those cries to the Queen of Heaven, the solemnity of the moment, all contributed to the splendor of the event."

Suddenly, interrupting her rosary, Lucy cried out: "There she is! I see her!"

Almost at the same moment, that immense multitude raised a cry of joy. Thousands of arms were lifted toward heaven. Mary gave a sensible proof of her presence.

"Look! Over there! There! Don't you see it? Oh, how beautiful!"

In the blue sky, not a single cloud could be seen; but soon, each one discovered the cause of this enthusiasm.

It was a luminous globe which, before these thousands of witnesses, was moving from east to west, gliding slowly, majestically, through space and emitting a bright but soft light, pleasant to look upon.

At the end of the usual time of the visions, the same globe was observed going up from the end of the Cova toward heaven, the direction from which it had come.

As for this prodigy, to be spoken of later, the one who most marveled was the vicar general of the diocese, who had come there incognito. Standing with a friend, some distance apart from the crowd, he observed this "airplane of light." His impression was that the globe served as a "vehicle" for the Mother of God, to bear her from heaven to the Cova da Iria and thence to bring her back to paradise.

Other unusual phenomena were noticed by the multitude during the vision. A white mist, perceptible to the very opposite end of the valley, surrounded the evergreen oak and the group of seers. At the same time, there fell from the sky what seemed like little white blossoms or flakes, which did not touch the earth but vanished at a certain height.

FIFTH INTERVIEW WITH THE LADY

During this time, Lucy and her cousins saw only the Lady. It was the fifth conversation of the little shepherds with the heavenly visitor.

She told them again to say the rosary in order to obtain the end of the war. *She promised to come back in October with St. Joseph and the Infant Jesus.* She insisted that they be there faithfully on the thirteenth of October.

Lucy asked the vision to cure many sick persons recommended to her prayers. She answered: *"I will cure a few of them, but not all, because the Lord does not trust them."*

This probably meant that their dispositions were too imperfect or that the cross of their trial was more salutary for them than their cure.

Speaking once more to our Lady, Lucy said: "The people would like to have a chapel here."

The apparition agreed to this proposal, adding that half the money collected should be used for the first expenses of the construction.

Though they knew that the seers conversed with an invisible being, the witnesses heard nothing of the mysterious voice.

Finally, Lucy declared: "Now she is going!"

Then the beautiful white mist vanished, the globe of light went up into the sky, the mysterious white flakes ceased to fall, the sun resumed its splendor and the atmosphere its clear light. The children went home with their parents who, trembling, had followed them at a distance.

INTERROGATIONS

The agreement of events with the children's predictions and the prodigies accompanying the visions increased Lucy's and her cousins' credit; but, even more, they excited public curiosity. Devout, curious, and wicked people, all came to question the little seers.

In August, Olimpia had taken the shepherding from her two younger children. Their brother John replaced them. In September, Maria Rosa sold all her sheep.

Some serious and competent persons also came to study these events. Among them was a learned priest, professor of theology at the Lisbon Seminary, Dr. Manuel Nunes Formigâo, Junior, who became the historian of Fàtima. By his kindness and amiability at his very first visit he won the good will of Aljustrel, and easily obtained frank and complete answers to all his questions. Without exception, these answers showed at once the candid, ingenuous souls of the three favored children.

8

THE SIXTH AND LAST APPARITION
(October 13, 1917)

POPULAR EMOTION AND EXPECTATION

Between the fifth and sixth apparitions, Lucy and her little cousins spent a few days at the neighboring village of Reixida. A lady of that village had obtained permission to keep them with her in order to withdraw them from the importunings of visitors.

But even there, curiosity seekers overtook them. The generous hostess said to her young guests: "Children, if the miracle you announce is not produced, those people could well burn you alive."

The little ones, who were always gay and amiable, answered: "We're not afraid! The Lady will not deceive us! She said there would be a great miracle and everybody would be forced to believe."

The accounts of thousands of the September pilgrims and the newspaper reports had spread widely the promise of a great miracle for the thirteenth of October. Truly, it would have been a terrible disappointment and, for many, the cause of an explosion of anger if it had not occurred.

The excitement was great at Aljustrel. Terrible threats were circulating. The children were exposed to great danger if the prodigy did not come. It was even whispered that a bomb was to be exploded near the children during the apparition.

The Martos were advised not to accompany their children on that day, but to let them go alone to the Cova. "They will not do them any harm, they are too small; but you might be ill-treated by the crowd."

44

On the eve, very early, Maria Rosa called her little girl. "My little Lucy, I think we'd better go to confession. They say that tomorrow, if the Blessed Virgin doesn't work the miracle, we must die at the Cova da Iria. The people are going to massacre us! Let's go to confession to be ready."

But Lucy was perfectly calm. "You go, Mamma, if you want to. I'll go with you, but I'm not afraid of death. What the Lady has promised will happen tomorrow."

Without being quite reassured the mother spoke no more of confession.

If the people persisted in talking of bombs to the children, they answered simply: "What a happiness it would be if we could go up to heaven with the Lady!"

All the day before, the roads leading to Fàtima are crowded with vehicles of every kind, without counting the pedestrians, many of them barefoot. In every group beads are recited and hymns sung. Despite the cool season, all these people are preparing to spend the night in the open air, to make sure of a good place the next day.

But the next day rises over all that region, cold, damp, and rainy. No matter, the crowd continually increases. They come from neighboring villages and from more distant towns. The newspapers of the capital have sent their best reporters.

The rain continues to fall all morning. Under this tramping multitude, the Cova da Iria becomes a vast puddle. Pilgrims and curiosity seekers are drenched to the bone. One might say that the vision has wished to test the faith of the pilgrims. But not one talks of going away.

About 11:30 the crowd has grown to *more than fifty thousand persons.*

All eyes are fixed on the place of the apparitions.

Lucy is happy today. Her mother and father are beside her. This time, Antonio and Maria Rosa have wished to accompany their daughter. "If Lucy is to die we shall die with her!" they courageously declare.

The multitude is so dense and so anxious to see the children that the latter would be crushed did not a few men form a body-guard about them. Besides, Antonio will not let go of his daughter's hand.

Seized with fear when she sees the crowds pressing them, poor little Jacinta begins to cry. Lucy consoles her, assuring her that nobody will hurt her.

Respectfully, as they draw near, people try to open up a passage for them.

The seers approach the evergreen oak, now only a hacked-up trunk. Their mothers have sought to beautify them today; the little girls wear blue dresses with white mantles.

A good lady of Pombalinho has embroidered flowers on their veils. Others have placed bunches of flowers in their hands and crowns upon their heads. The rain is still falling.

Pressed on every side, Jacinta cries and begs people not to push her. The two older children put her between themselves to protect her.

The beads are said. Between the decades popular hymns are sung and the echo of the hills catches, repeats, and amplifies the immense, suppliant, chanting voice that rises to heaven from the Cova da Iria.

THE MESSAGE OF THE "LADY"

Lucy asks the people to close their umbrellas. The order is transmitted at once through the multitude. Stoically it is obeyed.

At noon, precisely, Lucy starts and says: "The flash!"

Then looking toward heaven: "Here she is! . . . Here she is!"

"Look well, my daughter! Take care not to make a mistake!" says the mother, asking herself, not without anxiety, how all this is going to end.

But Lucy hears no more . . . ecstasy has seized her.

"The child's face," declared a witness at the inquest held on November 19, 1917, "was becoming more and more beautiful, with a rosy tint, the lips growing thinner."

Francis and Jacinta also perceive the Lady at the accustomed place.

While they are contemplating the vision, the crowd sees a little white mist forming three times around the group, then slowly rising into the air, like a cloud of incense floating away on high.

"Who are you, Madam, and what do you want of me?" questions Lucy.

The vision answers: *"I am Our Lady of the Rosary and I desire a chapel in my honor in this place."* For the sixth time she recommends that the beads be recited every day, adding that the war is about to end and that the soldiers will soon return home.

Then, Lucy, who had received so many supplications, says: "I have so many things to ask you!"

"I will grant some of them; the others,

And returning to the central point of her message, our Lady continues: *"Men must correct their faults and ask pardon for their sins."*

Assuming a sadder air, with a voice of supplication, she adds: *"In order that they no longer offend our Lord, who is already too much offended."*

These words remained strongly impressed on the children's minds. The sad look that overspread the Lady's face as she pronounced them will always be remembered. They were her last words, and they contained the essential point of the Fàtima message.

On bidding good-by to the children (who were persuaded it was the last apparition), with a gesture now familiar to them, she spread out her hands, which were reflected in the sun, as if she wished to turn the eyes of the children toward the daystar, now suddenly become visible.

THE DANCE OF THE SUN

At the very moment the Lady made this gesture, Lucy called out to the crowd: "Look at the sun!" (Her intention was not to direct the people's gaze to the solar phenomenon, but rather to the new vision, appearing next to it, to the astonished eyes of the seers. For all three at that moment beheld the Holy Family in the light of the sun.)

The whole multitude then witnessed a stupefying spectacle — never seen before — like one of those celestial prodigies which our Lord prophesied for the end of the world: "The powers that are in heaven shall be moved," the laws of astronomy will be overthrown.

Suddenly the rain stopped, and the clouds, dark and heavy since the morning, vanished. The sun appeared at the zenith, like a silver disk that the eyes could gaze at steadily without being dazzled, and at once began to turn on itself like a wheel of fire, projecting in every direction rays of light whose color changed many times. The firmament, the earth, the trees, the rocks, the group of seers, and the immense multitude seemed tinted successively with yellow, green, red, blue, and violet.

The sun stopped for a moment, then continued its change of light in a still more dazzling way.

It stopped once more and, a third time, these fantastic fireworks began, more varied, more colorful, more brilliant than ever.

How describe the impression of the crowd? Ecstatic, immovable, holding their breath, these seventy thousand seers gazed upward.

Suddenly, everyone without a single exception had the sensation that *the sun had been detached from the firmament and in zigzag bounds was coming down upon him.*

A loud cry broke from every mouth, expressive of universal terror. "Miracle! A miracle!" cried some. "I believe in God!" others proclaimed. Hail Mary was the prayer of many. Still more implored, "My God, have mercy!" and soon this last call became general.

A moment later, all those people had fallen on their knees in the mud and were reciting the act of contrition. One very old man cried out with hands extended: "Virgin of the Rosary, save Portugal!"

The rotation of the sun, with its intervals, had lasted just ten minutes. It was observed by all present, without exception: believers and unbelievers, peasants and townspeople, scientists, artists, journalists, even a good number of freethinkers. All, without preparation, without any suggestion but the call of a little girl to look at the sun, had perceived the same phenomena, with the same phases, on the day and at the hour announced a few months before as those of a great prodigy.

Later, the canonical inquiry on the miracle was to prove that the movements of the sun had been perceived by people who were three or four miles from the Cova da Iria, ignorant of what was going on there — not victims therefore of a collective hallucination.

The inquiry brought into relief another curious fact attested by all who were questioned on the subject. When the crowd had recovered from its stupor and could notice what was happening, *each realized that his clothes, which had been drenched by the rain and often spattered with mud, were now absolutely dry!*

These wonders were Mary's parting gift, not only to the children, but also to the Cova da Iria and to all the multitudes gathered there.

Therefore, the thought a thousand times expressed by that privileged crowd was: "We have seen the sign of God."

These miracles, doubtless too, were intended to show the importance the Mother of Mercy attached to the message she had brought to earth, through the mediation of the three little shepherds of Fàtima.

THE MULTIFORM VISION

The reader will remember our Lady's announcement that, during her last visit, she would bring St. Joseph and the Infant Jesus. That this promise had been realized for the little seers could be ascertained only by questions put to them after the general excitement had subsided.

Here are Lucy's words regarding this vision, which appeared not over the holm tree but in the sky, beside the sun, during the course of the solar prodigy: "I saw St. Joseph and the Infant Jesus beside our Lady. Then I saw our Lord blessing the crowd. Next our Lady showed herself, dressed like Our Lady of the Seven Sorrows, but without the sword in her heart. Finally, I saw her dressed in another way; I don't know how to say it, but I think it was like Our Lady of Mount Carmel. She was dressed in white with a blue mantle."

Like Lucy, her cousins had seen the Holy Family for a few minutes, but not the other visions.

"The Child was in the arms of St. Joseph. He was quite small, about a year old. They were both dressed in clear red."

The multiform vision had been unaccompanied by words.

AFTER THE SHOCK

Lucy, Francis, and Jacinta tried in vain to escape these thousands of witnesses. Everyone wanted to see them and attempted to speak to them.

In the crush, Antonio had to drop Lucy's hand. He saw her again only at the evening meal.

Her name was called right and left; over there in the wood; farther away at the meeting of the roads; then, in the pastorage, and even away off at Fàtima, in the square. They hunted for her at the Cova, at Aljustrel, in her home, and in the garden. He who succeeded in catching her, holding her, could only make her repeat what she had said so many times before. Some, hearing her describe the vision, wept like children. Others, without reason, expressed doubts. There were some who would deny it all, even the miracle they had just witnessed.

All those thousands had at last to go home. They returned to their dwellings and occupations, bringing with them news of the "sign" the Blessed Virgin had promised.

The next morning all the newspapers confirmed it in articles where the skepticism affected by the reporters ill concealed their profound emotion. For some days, in stores and in parlors, in markets and public places, there was no other subject of conversation than the events at Fàtima.

Portugal's centuries old devotion to Mary received from it all a profound and extraordinary impulse. Hearts seemed to feel the presence of the Queen of Heaven on the soil and in the air of Portugal. Hands touched the supernatural,

Soon, Fàtima's ray of grace will reach all nations, the whole world. Multitudes will open their eyes to the Infinite. Hearts will wake to true love, to Christian hope, to complete faith, because the Queen of Heaven answered the prayers of three little shepherds saying their beads, kneeling in the shadow of evergreen oaks.

9

INORGANIC PERIOD
(1917–1921)

AROUND THE WOODEN PORTICO

The thirteenth of October will always bear the stamp of a day memorable in the history of Portugal. The marvels of the Cova da Iria wrought a lasting impression upon all minds. From that day onward, innumerable pilgrims came to pray where Mary had made herself visible.

The rustic arch and the little rough stone wall that marked the exact spot of the apparitions had become a real sanctuary. Crowds of simple believers, without any organization, came from all directions to express their faith and love.

On workdays, they came singly or in little groups. But on Sundays and holydays, on the thirteenth of every month, especially from May to October, those little groups grew to thousands.

They were not urged to it by anyone. The vision herself had not asked, as Mary did at Lourdes, that there should be "processions"; yet the number of pilgrims grew more rapidly at the Cova than it had at the Grotto of Massabielle. They came spontaneously, hoping to share in the graces that Our Lady of the Rosary spread so abundantly, or simply moved by gratitude for some favor obtained or by sheer love for holy Mary. At all times, the beads were said aloud and hymns were sung with intense fervor.

The Lady had promised Lucy to cure some of the sick. She royally kept that promise. It would be impossible to relate the cures told one another by the pious pilgrims, between two rosaries, or sitting under the holm trees. Let us tell how only one pilgrim proclaimed his cure.

It was October 13, 1919. Around the little chapel, quite recently built, about six hundred persons knelt, while numerous other groups were seated on the surrounding hills, under the trees, resting or taking their meal. Suddenly, about fifty yards from the chapel, a large skyrocket shot through the air and burst with the noise of a cannon. After this, came a second, then a third and a fourth, up to twenty-one — a royal salute!

"Some pious people," writes Dr. Formigâo, "were complaining about this profanation of a holy place, which contrasted with the quiet recollection of the people. You could hear grumbling about the lack of interest shown by the clergy. If they had been there, this would not have happened! I thereupon went up to the man who had sent off the rockets, with a notebook and pencil in hand. 'Will you kindly tell me your name?' I said. He was surprised, grew pale, stiffened up, and answered: 'If you have the authority and want to arrest me because I sent off the rockets without permission, do your duty. I accomplished a vow and am ready to pay a fine for it, or even go to prison. I am ready for everything.'

"I quieted him, assuring him that I only wanted to know for sure whether that royal salute was merely the accomplishment of a promise. Then the good fellow brightened up, his face lit with enthusiasm, while in simple but eloquent words he told his touching story:

"He was a fireworks maker, and his workshop was in the suburbs of Porto-de-Mos. Last June he had been taken with a serious gastro-intestinal trouble. He lost all hope of human help; and, despairing at the thought of leaving his wife and children in absolute want, he turned to Our Lady of Fàtima and made the vow to send off a royal salute of twenty-one large rockets at the place of the apparitions, if he were cured. Immediately, he had begun to feel better and in a short time he was completely well. He had come today with his family to thank our Lady and to accomplish his vow."

The most striking miracles were performed in the depths of souls which, thanks to Mary, passed from unbelief or even hostility to fervor. It was so all through Portugal, a new pentecost, a resurrection of souls. Devotion to the holy rosary developed considerably without any help from the clergy who were forbidden by religious authority to work publicly for Fàtima.

Persecutors of the faith no longer dared to push their schemes. One often heard of wonderful conversions obtained by the invocation of Our Lady of Fàtima. Occasionally, too, the tragic death of someone was reported who, denying direct evidence, had blasphemed our Lady.

But Mary could sometimes take a more merciful revenge. One day a young man, of good family but little faith, accompanied his sisters to Fàtima. During the trip, one of the girls noticed that her brother was carrying a small bomb in his overcoat. Having reason to suspect his intentions, she managed to slip the bomb out while he was not looking, and replaced it with a set of prayer beads.

At the Cova da Iria they were mixed in with the crowd, but the sister carefully watched her brother's every gesture. What was her surprise to see him suddenly fall on his knees, crying and sobbing with emotion. Through Mary's intercession, grace had struck another irresistible blow.

In her last apparition, the Blessed Virgin had expressed to the children a wish to have a little chapel (*capelinha*) built at the Cova. Still, neither the parish priest of Fàtima, nor any member of the diocesan clergy, much less the patriarchate of Lisbon on which Fàtima depended, seemed to think of obeying this heavenly order. In the face of apparent insolvency, the pilgrims themselves began to build a chapel in the course of the spring of 1919. It was inaugurated on the twenty-eighth of April.

It was a modest edifice, a few square yards in area at the most, with a tiny square in front of it. What was that to contain the crowds that came like an irresistible avalanche? For the devotion of the Portuguese to the Virgin who had appeared at Fàtima was ever increasing.

The Church at Fátima (restored)

The Basilica From the Gate

— Courtesy Fàtima-Éditions

Schoolhouse in the Time of Francis and Jacinta

Lucy's House, Her Uncle Marto, and a Niece

— Courtesy Fàtima-Éditions

— Courtesy Fàtima-Editions

The Birthplace of Francis and Jacinta

The *Capelinha*, the Fountain, and the Women's Hospital

— Courtesy Fàtima-Éditions

Manuel-Pedro Marto and Chanoine Barthas at the Well
in Lucy's Garden

The Parish House at Fàtima

SECTARIAN OPPOSITION

One of the causes that increased popular devotion was the war let loose by hell against the new "superstition" — a war which, by the spontaneous reaction of popular faith, obtained a result quite contrary to what had been expected.

The sectarian forces of the country did not limit themselves to spreading ridicule and calumny by means of the press; they also had recourse to violence.

We saw how the subprefect of Ourém tried to prevent the apparition of the thirteenth of August, and we shall tell of the cruel trial he inflicted upon the little seers.

One month later another painful incident took place. Knowing that the local authority would leave them free, a band of ruffians came from Santarem in an automobile, to steal the *ex votos* and other objects left by popular piety at the spot of the apparitions. They overthrew the little portico, carried away various objects, and even wanted to cut down the holm tree and drag it away behind their car. They mistook the tree, however, since the relic was then only a bare stump, cut down a neighboring tree, and went off with it.

At Santarem they organized a nocturnal procession, seasoned with ribald songs and accompanied by blasphemous speeches, dragging through the streets the objects they had taken from the Cova. About a hundred took part in these shameful proceedings. No one dared intervene, knowing that behind these rowdies hid the official authority of the district, glad to see the "freethinkers thus strangle at birth these combinations so well-prepared to re-awaken the faith."

The local authority, too, dared to intervene directly. It asked the clergy, as well as the local magistrates, to forbid all gatherings at the Cova da Iria. Certain priests of the locality, in fact, had trouble with the administration.

But in spite of all that the movement of crowds toward the Cova was only increasing. Beginning with 1920, the central government itself sought to impede it.

The most notable episode, because of the forces brought into action as well as the fiasco in which it culminated, was that of May 13, 1920.

There was a first act played by the mayor of Torres-Novas. A young man of that town, recently converted, had ordered a statue of our Lady, made according to the description of the seers, to be placed in the little chapel of the Cova da Iria. When the statue came into the town it was received with enthusiasm by the faithful townspeople who came in crowds to admire it. This did not serve to diminish the alarm and fury of the freemasons. They called upon the mayor to order the giver to keep his statue and not to bring it to Fàtima. To make sure he was obeyed, the mayor had the house surrounded by policemen. But the statue did come out from the house and pass through the guards in an oxcart where it lay hidden under garden tools. Triumphantly it entered the Cova da Iria, and to this day our Lady receives before it the supplications and veneration of millions of pilgrims.

The central government took the lead in the second act. It gave orders to the surrounding townships to stop all vehicles going to the Cova da Iria. At sunrise, on the thirteenth, it placed squadrons of cavalry and troops of infantry around the Cova, to prevent approach to the place of pilgrimage. But the holy obstinacy of the pilgrims triumphed over everything. With their vehicles stopped, the pilgrims went on foot, pushed through the lines of soldiers, most of them good country folk who were quite willing to be overcome. Finally, a considerable number of them even begged of their officers and obtained permission to go and pray before the little oratory.

One of the officers thus expressed his feelings to the historian of Fàtima, Dr. Formigâo: "If you only knew how ashamed I am to be here. . . . I do what I am told to do, but, believe me, I hate it. I am a believer, and I see no advantage in preventing these poor people from coming to pray in this place." Then he added, with tears in his eyes, "I have a sister whose life Our Lady of Fàtima saved."

That day thousands of pilgrims found their way to the Cova.

They left it, more decided than ever to resist and protest against freethinking officials. But these would not withdraw. Their sectaries blew up the little chapel with dynamite during the night of March 6, 1922. It had lasted no more than three years. There was a surprising circumstance, however, which the people considered a heavenly intervention. Of the five bombs placed only one did not explode — the one set at the root of the shrub on which the Blessed Virgin had appeared.

This outrage raised a wave of indignation. It was strongly reproved even by the press. From all parts, even from parliament, protestations arose. Pilgrimages of reparation were immediately organized. One week after, ten thousand people walked from the parish church of Fàtima to the ruins of the chapel to make reparation.

But that was not enough — there had to be a national reparation. It took place on the thirteenth of May following, five years after the first apparition.

The governor of the district, wishing at any price to prevent what he called "a review of all the reactionary forces of the country," forbade all meetings. His subordinate, however, the new administrator of Ourém,* judged it more reasonable not to execute the orders of the overzealous governor, whose decision, moreover, was disavowed by his governmental chief.

The number of pilgrims was estimated at sixty thousand. They had come from every province and represented every social class and profession. Such a crowd had not been seen at the Cova da Iria since the day of the "sign of God."

The sight of the ruins of the little oratory, raised at the request of the Blessed Virgin, increased the fervor of all those people and prompted the offering of such sums of money that it was decided at once to build another chapel as soon as ecclesiastical consent could be obtained.

Certainly the hostility and violence turned to the glory of Fàtima.

---

* The former governor, known as "The Tinsmith," had been replaced by the government, had founded a Carbonari center (a "cell," communists would call it), and was hurt while making bombs.

The calumnies of the press had no better success. On the contrary, they became advertisements for the marvels that had occurred and were occurring there every day.

To the incredulous but one argument remained: the disappearance of the seers, for two of them, Francis and Jacinta, were already "in heaven." There was nothing suspicious or doubtful about their disappearance. They had been seen and questioned. Their sincerity could not be doubted.

Besides, none of three little shepherds ever saw the glory of Fàtima. Lucy herself was soon to leave Aljustrel to live far from the eyes of the world, "for God alone."

10

A PROVIDENTIAL PASTOR

A BISHOP, AT LAST!

He who, in the divine plan, was to be the chief author of this magnificence was the new bishop of Leiria, Msgr. José Alves Correia da Silva.

The head of this diocese had been appointed as recently as 1920. Born in 1872, the new prelate was forty-eight. He had been professor of theology in the Seminary of Porto, devoting himself also to the Catholic press and social action. He was one of the most persecuted of men in revolutionary times, since he had suffered grave vexations in more than one long imprisonment.

Our Lady of Fàtima could not have chosen one more worthy to execute her plans and be the apostle of her glory. The bishop of Leiria was most devout to Mary. He had already made ten pilgrimages to Lourdes and has made five more since his elevation to the episcopate. Enthroned on August 5, 1920, he solemnly consecrated his diocese to the Queen of Heaven, on the Feast of the Assumption.

He had a most difficult task ahead of him, to re-establish a diocese suppressed for more than forty years. There was but one thing concerning it that could give him consolation: it was the Cova da Iria where such manifestations of faith and piety had arisen. Little had been done to study the history and legitimacy of the new cultus of Our Lady of Fàtima, and that little had been done independently of ecclesiastical influence.

In 1917, the diocese of Leiria no longer existed; Fàtima depended upon the diocese of Lisbon. The cardinal patriarch, having heard of the first apparitions, had forbidden his clergy to meddle in any way with the events occurring there. However, the governmental persecutions obliged the cardinal to leave his diocese, and his vicar general was named administrator of the patriarchate.

It was to him that Manuel Ferreira, curé of Fàtima, addressed a letter on October 15, 1917, requesting him to inquire into the facts, of which he gave him a first-class account. On the third of November he received the order to proceed on his own initiative with the inquest. He set about it immediately, but so many witnesses were to be examined that the document was not ready until a year had elapsed. Actually his account was not transmitted to the patriarchate until April, 1919. In the meantime, Father Manuel Ferreira had been replaced by his cousin, Agostinho (Augustin) Ferreira.

In 1918 the diocese of Leiria was re-established, but its incumbent was not named for two more years. Two weeks after his nomination, Msgr. José da Silva received the documentary files concerning Fàtima, for which he now had the responsibility.

Prudently and wisely, Msgr. da Silva read or listened to all the accounts, favorable, neutral, or hostile. He reserved his judgment, however, wishing to arrive at a personal decision. He soon realized that he must take a definite stand. The facts of Fàtima were no light matter. Thousands of the faithful believed in the apparitions. On all sides marvelous cures were attributed to the intercession of the Blessed Virgin at the Cova da Iria. The Catholic people were almost unanimous in asking for an official declaration from the religious authority. The bishop must put an end, too, to the discussions of the clergy. He wished to finish with all these hesitations and doubts by deciding finally where the truth was. His confident love for the Queen of Heaven made him believe easily that Mary had chosen a humble spot of his own diocese to recall to men the way of salvation. And why would she not take for her messengers, as she had done elsewhere, humble and devout little shepherds? So, then, as soon as he was named bishop of Leiria, he began to study most carefully the visions that had prepared this new cultus and the miracles that popular faith connected with them.

More than once he personally questioned Lucy, the only one

now left of the three little shepherds. The answers of the young
girl were always simple and sincere. He could discover nothing
in them contrary to faith and the moral law.

Finally, overcome by the luminous evidence of the supernatural,
he decided to take upon himself the direction of this new cultus
that had spontaneously arisen at the Cova da Iria.

THE MIRACULOUS SPRING

At once, in 1921, Msgr. da Silva bought over thirty acres surrounding the place of the apparitions, more than twice the area
of the great piazza of St. Peter's at Rome. Under the direction of
his architects Cristino and Corrodi the work of construction began.

After building an encircling wall with monumental gates they
planned a chapel for Masses, a hospital for the sick, and finally a
great basilica.

Till then, the pilgrims had heard Mass and received the sacraments at the parish church, and then walked in procession as far
as the *capelinha*. That same year, on the thirteenth of October, the
kind prelate authorized the celebration of a Mass at the Cova da
Iria for the first time. It was said in the open air, before the little
chapel of the apparitions.

The Queen of the Rosary seemed to be waiting for this sign of
the bishop's approval to show her own good pleasure.

A few days after the first Mass was said, Msgr. da Silva ordered
the digging of a cistern to collect the rain water. The spot selected
was naturally the lowest point of the valley, the exact place where
the children stood for the first apparition. By this, the prelate merely
intended to facilitate the securing of water for the works of construction, and to provide for the needs of the pilgrims. The
Fàtima plateau, it should be said, is extraordinarily arid and so
water is a precious rarity. In the whole parish there is but one
spring, at Fonte Nova, in a deep ravine, below and far away from
the village.

Now, however, the workmen had scarcely begun to dig the
cistern when, to their astonishment, at the first few blows of the
picks, little streams of water began to flow. Soon all the rivulets

joined, forming a considerable stream. Before long this had filled the cistern under construction, not with rain water, but with clear, fresh spring water, sufficient for all the needs of pilgrims and builders. This event took place in November, 1921.

The people in that country all know that there was no water there before. The soil is calcareous, incapable of retaining the least humidity. Clearly, then, here was an evident "miracle of Our Lady," responding to the zeal of the holy bishop.

Soon, miracles like those at Lourdes were attributed to the use of this water, confirming the opinion of its supernatural origin.

Later, when the pilgrimages grew, Mary was to provide for the growing needs in the same way. In 1927, at a distance of some twenty yards from the first spring, workmen's picks caused a second spring, more abundant than the other, to well forth from the rocks. The water of both springs was collected in a large reservoir at the foot of the monument to the Sacred Heart, and there pours out from fifteen faucets at two different heights.

What maternal tenderness on the part of the Queen of Heaven! How, without that water, could those masses of half a million pilgrims gather at Fàtima? All the more, during the tremendous heat of summer?

OPENING OF THE CANONICAL PROCESS

Msgr. José da Silva did not allow himself to be completely absorbed in the material arrangements of the pilgrimage grounds. He wanted above all to give this place a doctrinal and canonical foundation.

On May 3, 1922, he published an ordinance prescribing a canonical process regarding the events at Fàtima. He named a commission of seven members, men of science and virtue, who should examine them from every point of view.

All the faithful of the diocese were obliged (those of other dioceses were invited) to give an account to this commission of all they knew, either in favor of or against the apparitions and other extraordinary facts. The work of the commission was carried out with scrupulous care and without haste. The investigation continued in fact throughout seven years, a long time for the devotees of Fàtima.

The commission presented its long account in 1929. Msgr. da Silva took six months to review it and to prepare his decision. This, then, was promulgated on October 13, 1930, thirteen years after the sixth apparition.

11

SANCTUARY BUILT — PILGRIMAGES ORGANIZED

THE FIRST PILGRIMAGES

The Christians of Portugal did not take long to manifest their love and devotion for Our Lady of the Cova. But for a considerable period there was no other sanctuary than the parish church, which stood more than a mile away. Hence many were satisfied to visit the *capelinha* when that was built. Only those who wanted to go to Holy Communion went to the church.

When, to the joy of all Portugal, the bishop had given leave to priests to preside at the prayers and to say Mass in the place of the apparitions (October, 1920), these ceremonies still were taking place in the open air, with whatever preparations could be made.

Little by little, however, in the old field of the Santos, avenues and terraces began to appear. Here and there walls were going up. The first building to be erected was a chapel intended mainly to make it possible for pilgrim priests to celebrate the Holy Sacrifice there, while awaiting the building of the projected basilica. It also contained confessionals for the pilgrims.

Soon pilgrimages were organized; whole parishes came with their clergy and various groups followed their chaplains.

It is truly a miracle that devotion to Our Lady of Fàtima should have drawn such constantly increasing crowds, with no direction or guide but Mary herself, and should have given rise to no disorder, no notable abuse, no superstition. This procedure continued for a period of four years.

"LA VOZ DA FÀTIMA"

On October 13, 1922, the first number of the "Voice of Fàtima," *La Voz da Fàtima,* appeared, the pilgrims' monthly paper published with the approbation of the diocesan authority. This date marks a real progress in the diffusion of Fàtima news.

The bishop's plan was to spread devotion to Our Lady of the Rosary; to keep an account of the pilgrimages, the miracles, and the favors granted; and retrospectively to relate the wonderful events of the year 1917.

The director of this publication was Dr. Marquès dos Santos, professor in the Seminary of Leiria. Its chief editor was (and still is) Dr. Nunes Formigâo, professor of theology at Santarem Seminary, who has published many articles on Fàtima. The magazine started with an issue of 3000 copies; by 1943, the monthly circulation had already run from 320,000 to 390,000 copies. For a population of only seven million inhabitants, that makes an average of about one copy for every four families. In a country like France it would represent a circulation of two and a half million copies. The reader can roughly estimate the many millions of subscribers a proportionate circulation in the United States would imply.

THE "SERVITES" OF OUR LADY OF FÀTIMA

As the number of pilgrims increased, so also did that of the sick who came to Mary to ask for consolation and help. Individual charity sought to lighten the difficulties of travel, but here, too, the necessity of organization soon made itself felt.

The construction of a beautiful hospital was attempted first. Volunteer stretcher bearers and nurses were grouped into an association, which in turn was erected into a confraternity as early as 1924. Another, the association for Married Ladies and Young Ladies, was approved in 1926.

Later on the two associations were united to form the Pious Union of the Servites of Our Lady of Fàtima. It comprises four different sections: (1) priests, (2) doctors, (3) stretcher bearers, (4) Servants of Our Lady. All these give their time and labor freely for love of the Blessed Virgin. There can be nothing but the highest praise for their abnegation and devotedness. It has been said that even if there were nothing at Fàtima that one might point to, this pure charity for the sick alone would supply a sufficient reason for saying: "In truth, the finger of God is here." On March 11, 1931, the Holy See approved the Pious Union and granted it many indulgences.

THE WAY OF THE CROSS

For ten years crowds had been coming to the Cova da Iria. The bishop of Leiria had bought the land, started the constructions, and approved the Union of Servites — even a *Pilgrims' Manual* had been published with his approval. But in all that time, no public official act had as yet been performed by Msgr. da Silva. This much desired event was at last to take place at the inauguration of the Way of the Cross, whose stations lined the principal way of access to the sanctuary.

The first station was erected at the crossroads of the village of Roguengo do Fétal, a little less than nine miles from the Cova. The others are located at equal distances, with the fourteenth station rising at the main entrance to the sanctuary esplanade. Each one is marked by a great stone cross. These crosses were built on the initiative and at the expense of the various parishes along the way. They wished thus to make the pilgrimage more devout for pedestrians, who are always very numerous, especially from Roguengo to the Cova.

The inauguration took place on June 8, 1927, and was presided over by the bishop himself. The procession formed at eight in the morning, stopping at every station to recite prayers and hear the bishop's little sermon, and did not reach the sanctuary until two o'clock in the afternoon. The bishop then said Mass and, despite the late hour, four hundred pious Catholics received Holy Communion.

PIOUS ORGANIZATIONS

Devotion to Our Lady of Fàtima was expressed by more than a visit to the sanctuary. After reaching their homes, the pilgrims did not cease to think of our Lady who had shown herself there, nor did they cease to pray to her.

To assure their perseverance many grouped themselves into an association called the Confraternity of Our Lady of the Rosary at Fàtima, whose statutes were approved by the bishop of Leiria on January 15, 1928. Its object is to work, pray, and suffer for the conversion of sinners; to make reparation for the social sins of nations and of people; to promote the keeping of the commandments of the Church, especially that relating to Sundays and holydays; to pray for the foreign missions and contribute to their support; to intercede for the souls in purgatory; to pray for the sick and for all spiritual and corporal necessities recommended to Our Lady of Fàtima.

The next year the hospital was built, with its special provisions for the sick.

Then came the movement of closed retreats, with its beautiful House of Welcome. Thanks to these retreats, the Cova da Iria has become a center from which sanctity flows throughout the whole country. In the first year of this movement two hundred people made closed retreats. During more recent years, in 1936, 1937, and 1938, these numbers grew to 835, to 950, and finally to over a thousand.

Retreats are arranged for the various special movements of Catholic Action, for the members of the Third Orders, for the St. Vincent de Paul Society, for students, professors, lawyers, and doctors. There are also retreats for the clergy, stimulated by the good example shown them on the part of the Portuguese bishops. Since 1934, all the bishops of the country follow their spiritual exercises here.

The Pious Union of the Fàtima Crusaders was founded in February, 1934, and was canonically erected on April 18 of that year. It is an auxiliary association of Catholic Action proposing to extend the kingdom of God by prayer and action. This association has obtained great success — after four years it can count five hundred thousand members.

On the twentieth anniversary of the apparitions, the bishop of

Leiria began to collect *The Golden Book*, in which were to be inscribed the names of families who sent their signatures, obliging themselves to say the rosary in common (or at the parish church with their pastor) each day. They also inscribe the names of those who promise to say it alone. The first volume, containing twenty thousand names, was offered to Our Lady of Fàtima in 1939.

12

THE HIERARCHY AND FÀTIMA

Until 1926, Fàtima had remained the particular affair of the little diocese of Leiria. Of course, people came from all the dioceses of Portugal; and, from time to time, especially on the thirteenth of May and the thirteenth of October, innumerable crowds were seen there. But from among the episcopacy, no other than the bishop of Leiria had ever appeared there publicly.

The first impulse was given by the archbishop of Evora, Dom Manuel Mendès da Conceiçào Santos, whose birthplace was Torres Novas, near Fàtima. In 1926 he came incognito to visit the sanctuary. His example bore fruit. The apostolic nuncio at Lisbon, Msgr. Nicotra, having come to Leiria to preside at a feast, asked to see the sanctuary at the Cova da Iria.

On descending from his car, however, the prelate beheld a spectacle that moved him deeply. Though it was not a pilgrimage day, about sixty persons were kneeling before the little chapel, praying with a fervor that could be seen only there. "It seemed as if our Lady were among those good people," said the prelate. He himself stayed there a good while in prayer, participating in the recitation of the rosary with the pilgrims. At last, deeply moved, the nuncio improvised a little speech and gave those present an indulgence of two hundred days.

Other episcopal visits followed until, finally, on May 13, 1931, all the Portuguese episcopate, under the direction of His Eminence, Cardinal Cerejeira, took part in the national pilgrimage in thanksgiving for the canonical approbation of the devotion to Our Lady of Fàtima.

THE BASILICA AND OTHER CONSTRUCTIONS

On May 13, 1928, the eleventh anniversary of the first apparition, the cornerstone of the great basilica was laid. The archbishop of Evora performed the ceremony. It was placed in the very same spot where the three little shepherds had amused themselves, "building a house," on the day Mary showed herself to them.

This splendid edifice was designed to be more than 280 feet long and 171 feet high, by far the largest church in Portugal. The main altar and fourteen side chapels were to recall the fifteen mysteries of the rosary.

At the present writing, one hundred workmen of all trades have been working for thirteen years at this monument of popular gratitude. Its enormous expense has been met by the gratuitous offerings of the faithful. They have paid, too, for the leveling of that arid, rocky plateau, for the construction of the encircling wall with its monumental gateways, and for other outlays.

Thus, little by little, this marvelous Marian city has arisen, by the strong will of one man who has understood that the Queen of Heaven wishes to possess, in this new sanctuary, a splendid monument to her glory and her mercy. All honor to the bishop of Leiria!

ROME AND FÀTIMA

In 1928 Fàtima was officially recognized in Rome.

Information published by *Osservatore Romano* on the new sanctuary and its pilgrimage acquainted Rome and the Vatican with Fàtima. Its impressive account of the grand assembly of May 13, 1928, was widely noticed, especially since it indicated that the Holy Father looked kindly at the new devotion.

The Portuguese College of Rome, that very year, built a new chapel to be blessed on the eighth of November. A statue of Our Lady of Fàtima, offered to the College by the sculptor himself, Joseph Ferreira Thedim, was to be placed above the main altar. This statue of oak is the most beautiful one existing, surpassing even that of the *capelinha*. It was blessed at the Vatican by the Holy Father himself. Pius XI remained a long time, studying the supernatural beauty of Our Lady of Fàtima. When, on the ninth of January following, the pupils of the Portuguese College came to offer their New Year's greetings to the Holy Father, he showed his esteem for Our Lady of Fàtima by giving them each two pictures of Thedim's work, one for themselves and one for their family, asking them to pray to Mary for the Pope.

One famous prelate did not hesitate to declare that this act of Pius XI would remain marked in letters of gold in the annals of Fàtima as an "implicit approbation."

The thirteenth anniversary of the first apparition was celebrated in the chapel of the Portuguese College. On that occasion, a decree of the Congregation of Rites was issued granting to every priest who would say Mass in this chapel the privilege of celebrating the Mass of Our Lady of the Rosary.

LAST OPPOSITION OVERCOME

By this time there was only one Portuguese prelate who still objected to the introduction of the devotion to Our Lady of Fàtima into his own diocese. It was the venerable bishop of Portalegre, Msgr. Domingos Frutuoso, of the Order of Friars Preachers. But after his visit *ad limina* all his hesitations disappeared. From that moment on, he authorized the devotion, blessed some statues, and solemnly inaugurated them.

According to certain rumors, his sudden change was due to a direct personal consultation with the Holy Father.

On March 25, 1931, the bishop of Portalegre presided at a great pilgrimage of his diocese to consecrate his seminary to Our Lady of Fàtima. In a few years its enrollment had grown from 32 to 180 students. Thus, the last of the opposing bishops was the first to pontificate in the sanctuary of Fàtima, for the devotion to the Virgin of the Cova had just been officially and solemnly approved.

13

PRODIGIOUS DEVELOPMENT OF THE PILGRIMAGE

CANONICAL APPROVAL

Rome seemed all along to approve of Fàtima; yet local ecclesiastical authority, while letting popular piety take its course, or even directing it, had not officially declared itself. The inquest opened by the bishop in 1922 was still under way thirteen years after the apparitions.

At Lourdes, at Pontmain, and at La Salette a decision had been reached within from one to five years after the apparitions. Why did it take so much longer at Fàtima? Doubtless because the supernatural events to be examined were particularly important and the judgment to be pronounced upon them required more consideration, more mature thought.

Finally, in 1929, the bishop had secured all the requirements for a final judgment. He spent the summer studying them and at last published his *Pastoral Letter on Devotion to Our Lady of Fàtima*, which has been called the Great Charter of Fàtima. It declares the apparitions of Our Lady at the Cova da Iria, from the thirteenth of May to the thirteenth of October, to be worthy of our belief, and authorizes the cultus of Our Lady of Fàtima. This pastoral letter was solemnly proclaimed at the Cova on October 13, 1930, in the presence of more than one hundred thousand faithful.

Thirteen years had elapsed since the last of the apparitions. Soon, on all sides, the idea of a great national pilgrimage of thanksgiving on the coming thirteenth of May was popularly expressed. The event itself finally took place in the presence of all the bishops of the country, presided over by Cardinal Cerejeira, patriarch of Lisbon. The vast assembly comprised at least three hundred thousand pilgrims.

LIKE AN IMPETUOUS TORRENT

Henceforth, nothing could prevent the development of popular piety for Our Lady of Fàtima, so that this, the youngest of our great Catholic sanctuaries, is still the most frequented.

Naturally it is to be expected that there will be fewer visitors during the winter months, not only because of the temperature, but because no anniversaries of the apparitions occur during this season. Yet, even on the worst days, there are about a thousand visitors, and on the thirteenth of every winter month, there are from one thousand to five thousand faithful who come to pray to our Lady.

During the months from May to October this number rises to a hundred, a hundred and fifty, and two hundred thousand, especially on the thirteenth of May and October. Then, the devotees of our Lady are not surprised to hear that three hundred thousand actually have prayed in what was once the field of Antonio dos Santos.

Yet it is no easy trip that brings one to the sanctuary. The nearest railway station is far below in the plain, ten miles away, so that cars, once rare in that country, are now much used. Government agents counted the cars in 1929 — there were eleven thousand. In May, 1934, there were fifteen thousand. In the anti-Communist pilgrimage, in 1938, there were twenty-eight thousand, and about two hundred and fifty thousand people were conveyed in them. If one counts those who went on foot, on bicycles, or in carriages, it is easy to believe there were *from four hundred and fifty to five hundred thousand* faithful praying at the Cova da Iria.

GENERAL APPEARANCE AND SPIRIT OF THE PILGRIMAGE

At Fàtima there is no convenience of any kind, not a single hotel or inn for those innumerable pilgrims. They are therefore true

pilgrims, animated with the spirit of penance so earnestly called
for by Mary herself in her words to Lucy and her cousins, and
echoed by the bishop of Leiria when he made his wise rules.

Here is one of the regulations published in *La Voz da Fàtima*,
on May 13, 1925:

"The pilgrimages to Our Lady of Fàtima must maintain their
primitive spirit of piety, penance, and charity. People come to
Fàtima to pray, to perform mortifications, to beg of the Virgin
Most Holy the physical or spiritual cure in body or soul of the
sick who come, ever more numerously, to throw themselves at the
feet of her who is truly *Salus Infirmorum*.

"Always and everywhere, especially on the way here and at the
Cova da Iria, the pilgrims must help each other, pray for one
another, be courteous to one another, and in all ceremonies keep
a respectful and deferential attitude.

"The sick, rich or poor, always hold the first place. Make room
for them and help them whenever necessary.

"The walled enclosure must be considered a temple, at least
during the duration of a pilgrimage. Keep silence or, if necessary,
speak low.

"Pilgrims must obey the directions of the Servites of Our Lady
of Fàtima, so that everything may be done in order. Lack of order
is displeasing to God and disagreeable to most of the pilgrims."

For sixteen years this advice has been followed faithfully. The
pilgrimage of Fàtima has remained one of intense prayer and
fervent penance.

The spontaneous manifestations of faith, of confidence in Mary,
of gratitude and supplication assume constantly new forms, according to the disposition of the group represented or the fervor of
the individual.

The methodical organization that religious authority has succeeded in imposing on the pilgrimage has not deprived this
religious people of their direct, almost innate, simplicity. Therefore,
one notices here a profound sincerity seen nowhere else.

AS SEEN BY WITNESSES

Strangers — not numerous at present because of international circumstances — say they have seen nothing to be compared with Fàtima, either at Lisieux, at Rome, or even at Lourdes, as regards numbers, edification, or profound and fervent faith.

Dr. Ludwig Fischer, a Bavarian priest, professor at the University of Bamberg, was so enthusiastic over his first visit to Fàtima that he declared its marvels to his own countrymen. After May 13, 1929, he wrote: "It was a unique spectacle. At Rome, I had assisted at the canonization of St. Thérèse of the Child Jesus. I saw eighty thousand people there, filling St. Peter's and overflowing into the gigantic plaza. But what was that compared to this immense multitude filled with the spirit of sacrifice, with devotion to the Holy Mother and to the Blessed Sacrament."

The learned professor then described the splendors of that day. He was especially moved by the procession of Mary's statue and by the candlelight procession.

Another witness was Père Gonzague Cabral, S.J., who took part as preacher in the national pilgrimage of 1930. Writing to a friend, he said: "I never could have imagined what I witnessed here. I do not believe human words, written or spoken, could do justice to this experience. One has to see it. I had read, some time before, *Fàtima, das portugiesische Lourdes,* by Dr. Fischer. It is a remarkable book, the best, to my view, of those published on the subject. . . . But after seeing Fàtima, I must confess, nothing I read there comes up to what I saw. That day, I had before me an audience of two hundred and perhaps three hundred thousand pilgrims."

On May 13, 1932, Msgr. Jean Bede-Cardinale, then apostolic nuncio at Lisbon, was equally impressed. After the ceremonies at which he himself had presided, he made the following declaration:

"I confess I have never assisted at a spectacle such as Fàtima offered on the thirteenth of this month.

"That enormous multitude acclaiming the Blessed Virgin with intense faith and love, a multitude in which all race distinctions disappeared, because all felt they were sons of the same Mother and all were one in invoking her and honoring her, was a thing that moved the heart and made on the mind a profound, unforgettable impression.

"At Fàtima, there is nothing human to attract one. The pilgrimage itself is a real sacrifice. Despite that, the number of pilgrims grows daily. It is an interior force that draws them to this blessed spot where the Virgin Mary dispenses her favors, where souls come in great numbers back to God, whence all draw spiritual strength which, while renewing their energy and strengthening their will, helps them to persevere in the practice of Christian virtues.

"Fàtima is a true blessing for Portugal. I am convinced that Mary will always protect this nation whose thousand years of history recall so many truly Christian glories, and that she will protect it from those dangers which now threaten society throughout the world."

OUTSIDE OF PORTUGAL

Devotion to Our Lady of Fàtima is spreading rapidly throughout the nations. It is found in Spain, which has already sent pilgrimages to Fàtima; in France, Belgium, Holland, Switzerland, Italy, Malta, Austria, and Hungary. In Germany, before the war, there were several centers of devotion and pilgrimages encouraged by the "Fàtima Messenger" (*Bote von Fàtima*). A printing press in Bamberg worked especially for the diffusion of devotion to Our Lady of Fàtima in the German tongue. In Poland, at Tlumacz, in May, 1937, a Marian Congress in honor of the Virgin of Fàtima brought together from thirty to forty thousand Ukrainians.

Outside of Europe, the Virgin of Fàtima has churches, chapels, oratories, and altars: in the Azores, from Cape Verde to Madeira; in Eastern and Western Africa (Guinea, Belgian Congo, Portuguese Congo, Angola, Zululand, Mozambique, Tanganyika); in India (Goa, Cochin, Diu, Damâo, Bombay, Meliapore, Honavan, Pallaveram); in Singapore; in China (Macao, Toulown-Tong, Fouchou-Nantai); in Japan (Kobe); in the United States (Newport); in British Guinea (Georgetown); in Trinidad; in Brazil (Rio de Janeiro and Sao Paolo, Bahia, Pernambuco, and elsewhere); in distant Oceania (Timor, New Zealand, Hawaii) — everywhere, the Blessed Virgin spreads her marvels.

In the missions, among the pagans, there are many centers established under the invocation and the protection of Our Lady of Fàtima. The first was established at Ganda in Angola. Under the protection of Mary it developed so prodigiously that they could open a seminary for the natives. The church became a center of pilgrimages where the new Christians imitated what was done at Fàtima.

In Mozambique a cathedral is to be consecrated to Our Lady of Fàtima. This is only to show in a few words the wonders accomplished by the Portuguese missioners with the help of the Madonna of the Cova da Iria.

14

A DAY AT FÀTIMA

THE PILGRIMS' ARRIVAL

For a Catholic, there is no scene to be compared to the Cova da Iria on the thirteenth of May and the thirteenth of October of each year.

From the day before — the pilgrims arrive at Fàtima in the evening — all the roads and paths of the mountain are like rivers that pour their streams into the valley once visited by Mary. In the midst of thick clouds of dust come interminable processions in which, with fervor, the rosary is said and hymns are chanted.

In Portugal, many provincial and even local costumes can still be seen. All these groups approaching, variously clad, would give one the impression of an immense parade. It is also a veritable procession of all the means of locomotion, past and present. There are, first, a great number of pilgrims drawing near on foot — interminable files of people of every age and condition, walking, walking, walking, for twenty-four hours, for forty-eight hours, and more. Many are barefoot, carrying footwear in their hands, around their neck, or in a bag.

Some have walked two hundred or two hundred and fifty miles, taking eight or ten days or even more to come from the other end of the country.

Others have arrived on horseback, on bicycles, in old-fashioned jaunting cars, and even in haycarts, drawn by phlegmatic oxen who move peacefully through this bewildering confusion.

In the midst of all this can be seen in contrast automobiles, trucks, tourist cars, and luxurious limousines.

The first thing a pilgrim does on arriving is visit the *capelinha* which, on the very spot of the apparitions, preserves the statue of the Madonna at the identical place where she set her feet.

Few are the eyes that are not wet with tears at that recollection. The Virgin is there, in a corner of the edifice. She welcomes kindly, maternally, all those children whom she knows, whom she expects. They, too, know their Mother. With what faith, with what tears of joy do they salute her. They speak to her, invoke her aid, and actually wrest graces from her. Mothers raise up their little children that their tiny hands may touch the Blessed Virgin. Each pilgrim brings some pious object to touch the statue and then takes it away. with him, a supernatural reminder of this precious moment.

One sometimes sees pilgrims, sometimes whole families, going around the chapel on their knees. Despite their good will, in this immense crowd, people push against them, are thrown upon them, or walk over them. They keep on. They have made a promise; they want to gain a favor. Some leave the ground marked with blood from knees wounded by the pebbles on the way.

Darkness is falling. When will that multitude seek rest? But who cares for that? None have sought restaurants for the evening meal or even a room to sleep in. Each one continues his or her devotions. Each one has so much to ask of the Blessed Virgin; each has so many messages for those who could not come.

THE PROCESSION BY CANDLELIGHT

The clock strikes ten. Up to that hour the solemn valley has looked like a lake whose human waves are moved by a great tempest. Now the aspect changes. Here and there, in the semidark- ness, appear little points of light. Let us read Father Fischer's description:

"I was standing where the basilica is now, whence my eye took in not only the holy enclosure, but also the surroundings, like a vast amphitheater. Suddenly, in the darkness little luminous points appeared. In a moment they became hundreds, the hundreds be- came thousands and tens of thousands; in a few minutes, the somber glen had become a sea of vivid flames.

"An extraordinary, unique spectacle that has not its equal in the world. I have seen the tapers of Kevelaër, of Einsiedeln, of Altötting. I have seen those of Lourdes, too. But what are they compared to that ocean of fire?

"That resplendent May night in the Cova da Iria surpasses all one can imagine. It is truly a holy night of light in the midst of a world plunged in the darkness of sin."

His Excellency the Bishop of Leiria soon arrived. That was the signal for the torchlight procession. Procession is just a way of speaking. To proceed comfortably, that gigantic crowd would have required miles and miles of avenues. Nevertheless, the compact mass of people organized itself into a kind of luminous serpent that wound its links as best it could in the too narrow space offered by the Cova.

They prayed, sang, and acclaimed the Virgin. In the center of the Cova, a priest, standing before a microphone, directed the prayers, songs, and acclamations. Powerful loud-speakers on all sides repeated his words, so that those two hundred thousand voices answered together in perfect order.

Midnight was drawing near when the procession closed with the chanting of the *Credo*. This tremendous choir of hundreds of thousands of voices, in the light of a like number of tapers, was truly sublime. "The spirit of the catacombs dwells there: the revenge of faith, eternal and holy, over the errors and ugliness of a corrupt world." It is the triumph of our ancestral faith, the faith of Nicea and of the Apostles in the radiance of the Virgin Mother. This spectacle has often touched and converted tourists who had come there simply drawn by a movement of curiosity. In 1927 a famous professor, assisting for the first time at this procession, exclaimed: "Truly, if Mary had appeared, they could not have received her better."

NOCTURNAL ADORATION

Midnight! The pilgrims begin the nocturnal adoration, usually presided over by the indefatigable bishop of Leiria. Standing before the microphone, he directs the rosary, adding before each decade an explanation of the corresponding mystery. He does it in words inflamed with love and devotion for Mary.

Between times, he indicates the intentions: the sovereign pontiff, the bishops, Portugal, the sick, all the pilgrims' intentions and those that others have recommended to them. And those thousands of hearts, beating like one in perfect charity, quivering with holy fervor, are fused into one unanimous prayer. That is the true Communion of Saints.

It is two or three in the morning. The care of adoring the Blessed Sacrament and of honoring Mary is to be confided to different diocesan delegations who will replace one another in these nocturnal prayers, each watching one hour while the other groups rest a little.

The greater number of pilgrims just lie down on the ground; others use their cars.

Everyone does not sleep, however. The men, who alone are admitted to the confessionals during these night hours, form long ranks before the twenty "boxes," for four or five hours patiently waiting their turn.

One evening, Msgr. da Silva, coming out of the confessional where he had spent long hours, was accosted by a woman.

"My Lord, for the love of God, won't you hear my confession?"

"The night *Angelus* has rung, we confess only men now."

"Poor me! I have been waiting ever since morning. I am going to Communion, and I must leave at once!"

"Are you still fasting?"

"Yes, certainly, my Lord."

"Well, there are no rules that hold, then!" cried the Bishop. And returning to the "box," he heard the confession of that patient soul, come, God only knows, over how many miles. Then he gave her the eagerly desired Holy Communion.

Yet such stories are not rare.

COMMUNION MASS

At earliest dawn, a Mass is said for the Servites who, in the morning, will be ready for their charitable work.

Then hundreds of priests offer up their Masses, following one another at the different altars. One altar is raised at the top of the steps leading up to the basilica still under construction. It can be seen from the whole Cova.

There, at about seven o'clock, one of the bishops present says Mass for the general Communion. Every one of that vast attendance will follow it piously and actively, thanks to the megaphones. The whole Cova is a huge temple with the blue sky for a dome.

The hymns of the *Schola Cantorum* intervene with the prayers of the multitude.

At the moment of Communion, twenty-five priests draw near to the altar with ciboria of ordinary size, to draw the Bread of Life from the large ciboria used for the consecration, each about a foot in diameter and containing six thousand hosts. Then they go in every direction to the immense crowd, distributing Holy Communion. Whoever wishes to receive Communion goes down on his knees in the mud or dust, and the priest who passes gives him the Bread of Life.

At the microphone during this time, the Schola chants the melody whose incomparable charm, once heard at the Cova, is never forgotten.

> Holy Angels and Archangels, Ah! keep us company!
> Help us to glorify the Eucharist Divine.

Indeed, the angels and archangels must come in glorious flights, while that immense multitude, filled with the holiness of the moment, cries out with devout enthusiasm:

> Hail to Jesus in the Blessed Sacrament.
> Hail to Jesus, our Lord.
> Hail to Jesus, our Father adored.
> Hail to Jesus, who is our Love.

Father Fischer writes: "A large number of faithful, who had been waiting at least two hours in the burning rays of the sun, begged me to give them Communion. I went up to the altar with all the joy and happiness of a young deacon, going for the first time to touch the Body of his Lord. Whence comes this joy? Ah! Fàtima is a place of grace! Everything here is different from everyday life.

"I advance, ciborium in hand. The people make way, leaving a free passage. Men, women, and children, those from the city and those from the country, fall on their knees in the dust or the mud, wherever they are, as soon as the Eucharistic God draws near.

"Their great fear is that there might not be enough hosts. From all sides, they call out to me, whispering: 'Father! Father!' I admire that faith, that hunger for Jesus, that mutual charity, that anxious carefulness lest anyone should miss this sacramental coming of the Lord to his own breast.

"That day, more than twenty-five thousand Communions were distributed on the mountain of Fàtima."

In the following October, the Holy Communions were even more numerous, about forty thousand. This number has been surpassed many times: in May, 1931, the thirty-three thousand Communions took three hours, and in the anti-Communist national pilgrimage, forty-five thousand Communions were distributed by fifty priests.

PROCESSION OF THE BLESSED VIRGIN

Noon — it is the hour when, at six different times, Mary showed herself to the little shepherds; the hour when thousands of witnesses assisting at the apparitions saw the atmospheric phenomena accompanying them. It is the most fervent hour for the Fàtima pilgrims. In the surroundings of the Cova it is the hour of the grandest, most touching spectacle of faith to be witnessed in this world.

The statue of our Lady, which is kept in the Chapel of the Apparitions, is now solemnly borne to the high altar where the Mass for the sick is to be celebrated. Each time, this procession is marked by new proofs of love and enthusiasm.

In the *capelinha*, four Servites of Our Lady are ready to bear her wonderful statue on their shoulders, and the retinue is formed. First come the scouts, who with difficulty open a passage through the crowd; for so many are eager at this moment to draw nearer

to the blessed image of the Queen of Heaven, as if they must
speak to her close at hand and more confidentially. Then, floating
in the air, come the banners of the different groups of pilgrims.
Next, the clergy, and finally, the miraculous statue. The procession
advances slowly, very slowly.

Father Fischer again writes: "As soon as Mary's statue appeared
in the brilliant light of the sun, a shower of roses such as I had
never seen before began to fall. In the twinkling of an eye, the
statue and its bearers were covered with perfumed petals.

"Roses, however, do not grow in these wild mountains. The
pilgrims bring them for this solemn moment. Such an act must
be most agreeable to our Lady.

"We had scarcely gotten over our surprise, when a friend whispered: 'Look behind you.' I looked. We seemed to be suddenly in
a great field of snow. The whole valley, from its depth to its
extreme limit, gleams in the blinding noonday sun, all white with
handkerchiefs by the thousands and tens of thousands, which the
pilgrims are waving to salute the Virgin Mother! It is a magnificent sight such as only the Cova da Iria can present.

"Refuge of sinners! Health of the Sick! Mother of Mercy! Our
Lady of Fàtima! These are the cries that rise on every side.

"All cannot approach the miraculous statue, but their salutations
traverse the air, coming like angelic flights from the hearts of the
children to the feet of their Mother.

"Oh! the Cova da Iria! If it did not exist, it would have to be
created!

"Antique paganism invented the amphitheater, where evil celebrated its triumph. The new paganism, imitating the old, has its
stadium, its amphitheater. The devil is always the same and directs
his assaults preferably against the multitudes.

"The stadium where Mary triumphs today is the grand amphitheater of nature herself in the Cova da Iria. She is acclaimed there
as nowhere else: Conqueror of sin and of hell, Immaculate Lily
of virginal purity, Queen of heaven and earth, she who has crushed
all the heresies of the world.

"This incomparable spectacle was still going on, the procession slowly advancing, the handkerchiefs fluttering like snowflakes, when the same kindly voice whispered: 'Look now, everybody is weeping!'

"It was so. All this multitude, as if electrified by radiations from the miraculous statue, was struck by a mysterious tremor and could express its feelings in no other way than by tears.

"I looked about me. Far as I could see, there were tears in all eyes: men, women, priests, even the bishops on the steps waiting for the statue were in tears.

"Explain, whoever can, the tears in every eye. No marvel if the women above had cried. But men also, by the thousands, are breaking into tears, abundant tears: an inexplicable sight. I saw it only once in my life, on the 13th of May, 1929, in the Cova da Iria.

"In its own way, Fàtima is a unique sanctuary. There is only one Fàtima in the whole world."[*]

THE MASS OF THE SICK

The triumphal cortege advances to the basilica. There the statue enters the space reserved for the sick. We can see them gathered at the foot of the steps, lying on mattresses or seated on benches, sheltered from the ardent sun or the abundant rain by great awnings spread above them. It is what has been called "the sick people's enclosure."

Their prayerful, confident eyes are turned toward the blessed image that now will soon be placed beside the altar.

Mass begins. In unison the people sing the *Credo*. Then the faithful are invited to unite their prayers with those of the cele- brating bishop, for the conversion of sinners, for the sick present there, and for all the intentions recommended to the pilgrims. The rosary is recited for all these intentions.

When Mass is finished, the Blessed Sacrament is brought to each one of the sick, as is done at Lourdes during the afternoon procession.

Only the gravely sick are admitted into the walled space, gen-

---

[*] Fischer, Dr. L., *Fàtima, das portugiesische Lourdes* (1930).

erally those pronounced hopeless by the doctors. Only from three to five hundred are admitted here each time, and tens and hundreds must be refused admission tickets. Carrying the ostensorium, the bishop passes through the rows of sick, blessing them one after the other. What fervor in their looks and in their prayers! All the people gathered there pray with them and for them.

During this time, before the microphone, a priest, generally Dr. Marquès dos Santos, vice-rector of the diocesan seminary, pronounces the invocations and acclamations prescribed by the bishop: "Lord, we love Thee!"

And the echo, like a great roll of thunder, repeats that cry of profound affection rolling from fifty thousand throats: "Lord, we love Thee!"

A second and a third time the cry is repeated with an indescribable crescendo of fervor. Then, in the same way, the other invocations roll out.

Benediction of the Blessed Sacrament for the whole gathering closes this ceremony.

THE CLOSING

It is time now to think of our departure. But first, everyone stops where he happens to be. Few even think of sitting down. They listen to the instruction which serves also as the parting address.

Next, Mary's statue is brought back to the *capelinha*. This time it is carried by the ladies, Servants of Mary.

The people's enthusiasm, as Mary passes the second time through their ranks, is as great as during the procession. The white handkerchiefs are once more waved above their heads, with even more ardor than before, because each one wants to salute Mary's image before it disappears into the *capelinha*.

Near delirium is reached when it is reported that our Lady has granted some cure or some exceptional favor. For Our Lady of the Rosary keeps her promise to hear the prayers and to cure some of the sick. The *Bureau of Authentication*, under the leadership of the bishop of Leiria, has often registered true miracles, recognized after minute and persistent enquiry. In 1934, *La Voz da Fàtima* had already published the account of more than four hundred of these miracles. Actually, more than eight hundred had been published by 1943.

Each great day at Fàtima is the occasion of some extraordinary cure. The crowds of pilgrims seek to thank Mary by touching manifestations before once more dividing into moving streams along the various roads leading homeward, their souls still filled with the sweet emotions gathered at the feet of their heavenly Mother.

15

BEFORE THE APPARITIONS

FAMILY EDUCATION

Before the events of 1917, life for the three children chosen by Mary to be her messengers was serene and joyful in the peaceful and deeply religious surroundings of their homes.

They belonged to families rich in children. Their parents were not among those who fear to give new life. They considered every new cradle a gift from heaven.

Francis and Jacinta, ninth and eleventh children of Olimpia, did not enjoy this world's happiness very long. They barely appeared in it. But they are now the honor and glory of all Portugal and the whole Catholic Church, and their surviving parents and relations have the assurance that they are unspeakably happy in heaven, since Mary — of that they are certain — came to call and take them.

It may seem surprising to read that the three little seers had never gone to school. Men's first thought in that country is to painfully cultivate the ungrateful soil, and then care for the flocks. In large families, only one or two are given the opportunity to be instructed, so that they can read to the family in the long evenings and do the necessary correspondence.

But for all that the education of children was not neglected. The home was the great school and the mother the true educator. Usually, neither Maria Rosa nor her sister-in-law went to work in the fields; they stayed at home to do the housework and the cooking. In free moments, they would spin or weave at the rough loom and take special care of the younger children.

They taught them their prayers and their catechism as soon as the little ones could learn. From the lips of her mother, Lucy, like Francis and Jacinta, learned to know and love our Lord and His holy Mother.

It was in the long evenings that the true education of the children was carried on. Then along with the catechism, the parents taught them country and family traditions, the rules of life, the songs of the land, the principal events of their national history, and whatever else may have been of special consequence to them.

Lucy loved to hear her mother tell about the lives of the saints or stories from the Gospel, rather than to hear her elder sisters or her father tell fairy tales and stories from profane history.

She, who later was to be judged by some as foolish, profited so well by her mother's lessons that before reaching the age of seven she was allowed to make her First Communion. This favor was granted her because a passing preacher, Father Cruz, S.J., examined her himself, was astonished at her answers, and insisted that she should be admitted to Holy Communion.

INNOCENT FRIENDSHIPS

At these family catechism instructions, held sometimes in Maria Rosa's home, sometimes in Olimpia's, the three children often came together. There Francis and Jacinta became very friendly with Lucy, and soon preferred her company to any other. Their mothers had wished it so, because they were afraid their little ones might make contact with some ill-bred children, and had forbidden their playing with them.

They would often go to their cousin Lucy's and ask her to bring them to the well at her house. This well was hidden in the garden, among the olive and chestnut trees. A big stone slab covered it. They used to play there often, usually letting Jacinta choose the game, or repeating to one another the stories heard in the evening by the hearth. And hours would pass quickly.

Later, in the days of sorrow, they went there again — how many times — to pray and weep.

But now all is joy; everything smiles and sings around them and in their innocent hearts. If they hide "behind the well," it is to enjoy their happiness more fully.

It often happened though that less well-trained children of the hamlet came to trouble their solitude. When neighbors had to take a trip, they would often leave their children in the Santos' yard. Lucy would have to entertain them, under the eye of her two older sisters, who did the family sewing inside the house. So the yard and the enclosed space beyond were transformed into a little "kindergarten" where Lucy, then barely eight years old, acted as the "nurse."

On those days, since they could not go to their little "retreat," Francis and Jacinta rather sadly resigned themselves to playing with the others.

Sometimes, especially during Lent, Lucy's mother would call all the children indoors to teach them a little catechism. Once it happened that one of the boys had evidently used improper language. Maria Rosa severely reproved the culprit in the presence of all the others.

"Those naughty things should not be said," she told him. "They are sins that offend the Infant Jesus. And those who do not confess them go to hell."

The children were much moved, especially Jacinta. Henceforth, the three cousins kept pretty much together, so that their friendship steadily grew deeper.

FIRST SIGNS OF PIETY

The games these children played were very innocent. They were especially fond of "forfeits," in which the loser had to carry out the order of the winner. Jacinta, when she won, would command the other to catch a butterfly for her or bring her a favorite flower.

One day they were playing this game in Lucy's house. The latter won, and ordered Jacinta to kiss one of her brothers, who was sitting at the table writing.

"No, not that! Tell me something else. Why don't you make me kiss our Lord, who is over there?" And she pointed to the crucifix on the wall.

"You are right. Get up on the chair — bring it here. Now get down on your knees and kiss it three times, once for Francis, once for yourself, and once for me."

"For our Lord I will do it as often as you want!" And she kissed the crucifix with so much fervor that Sister Lucy still affirms she can never forget that sign of love.

Then the child, looking fixedly at the image, asked: "Why did the good Jesus die thus, nailed to a cross?"

"Because He died for love of us."

"Tell me about it."

Lucy hastened to do so. It was sufficient for her to have heard a story only once to repeat it almost word for word. It was not hard for her to satisfy her cousin. Jacinta, on hearing of the sufferings of our Saviour, was profoundly touched, even to tears. Later on, Lucy often had to tell her two cousins "the story of Jesus." Each time Jacinta would break into tears.

"Our poor Lord!" she would say, "I will never sin any more! I do not want to make the good Jesus suffer."

One year, at Corpus Christi, Lucy was chosen to be dressed as an angel and to throw flowers before the canopy at Jesus in the Host. As soon as Jacinta heard of it she asked for the same favor.

The lady who was to dress the "angels" was Lucy's eldest sister. Needless to say, she satisfied her little cousin. At the rehearsal she explained how the flowers were to be thrown toward Jesus in the Blessed Sacrament.

"And we shall see Him?" asked Jacinta.

"Certainly. The pastor is to carry Him."

The child leaped with joy. Afterward, many times a day, she asked when the great feast would come.

The much-desired day at last arrived, and with it came our two *anjinhos*, clothed in white and sparkling with gilt paper, their little baskets full of flower petals. At the given signal, the other "angels" also came along. Lucy threw her handful of flowers and signed to Jacinta to do likewise. But the little one did nothing but look steadily at the pastor bearing in his hands the beautiful ostensorium.

"Why didn't you throw flowers at Jesus?" asked Lucy's sister.

"Because I didn't see Him. Did you see the little Jesus?"

"Don't you know that the Infant Jesus in the Host isn't seen? He hides Himself. That is why we can receive Him in Communion."

"When you go to Communion, do you speak to Him?"

"Certainly."

"And how is it that so many people at the same time can receive Jesus hidden? Is there a piece for each one?"

"Well, no! There are many hosts and each host contains the Infant Jesus hidden."

Lucy's science, at this time, would have made a theologian smile, but Jesus certainly smiled still more with divine satisfaction.

Jacinta continued: "I'll ask Mamma if I may make my First Communion."

"The pastor won't allow you to until you're ten years old."

"But you aren't ten years old, and you have made it."

"Because I know my catechism well. Francis and you don't know it well enough yet."

So the two children asked Lucy to teach them. They set about studying their catechism so ardently that they forgot their games. And soon they had learned all their young catechist could teach them about the Holy Eucharist.

"Teach us something else," they would say. "We know that already." Finally it was decided to ask their mother Olimpia to let them follow the pastor's catechism classes at the church.

BEHIND THE FLOCKS

Lucy was now eight years old. Her sister Caroline, who had been looking after the flock, went to work in the fields since she was thirteen, and Lucy was ordered to replace her. She went to tell her cousin the news.

"Oh! then we won't be able to play together any more!"

The youngsters could not agree to this separation. They begged Mamma Olimpia to let them follow the new shepherdess through the hills and valleys, behind the flock. The permission was refused. But the children insisted so that, in the end, Mrs. Marto decided to let them keep a few sheep which up to then had been confided to an older sister. Then the three little shepherds arranged to combine their flocks and spend the day together.

A charming detail, which shows the careful training Olimpia had given them, is that Francis and Jacinta never set out with their sheep before reciting the Our Father and Hail Mary in honor of their guardian angels.

Now every day was a kind of holiday, spent running through the woods and over the prairies. Lucy, who knew the paths and mountain pastures better, would choose the direction to be taken.

About noon they usually found a nice shady place for breakfast (the Portuguese, like the French, take only a drink and a piece of bread in the morning, and breakfast at noon) and for the noonday *siesta* or rest. The light meal, prepared by the mothers with rye bread, cheese, and olives, was quickly consumed. After that they said their beads, a practice they had been told to observe punctually every day, after their noonday meal. But, in the hurry of play or of collecting blackberries in the shrubs, it sometimes happened that they skipped beads by saying only the first two words, "Hail Mary." Thus, in a few minutes, they were rid of the double duty of obedience to Mamma and of piety to our Lady.

With the new life, the games changed too. They loved to "build houses" with the stones of the mountain. Jacinta called for hymns, especially those in honor of Mary: "Hail, noble patroness" — "Angels, sing with me." If they met an older shepherd who had a flute or an accordion, they would ask him to play his instrument, so that they might dance a few steps. Jacinta, especially, loved music and dancing. She had a special talent for dancing which she was quite willing to display.

She loved, too, to hear the echo of her voice from the bottom of the valleys. She would make her companions stop at a suitable place, and there, sitting on a rock, they would fling at the echo all the names they could think of. The one which came back most clearly was: *Maria.* Jacinta would cry it out very often. Sometimes, she hurled out the whole *Ave Maria*, word after word, so that the echo itself prayed to our Lady. Yes, she said it in Latin! The

Portuguese, like the Italians, learn the most familiar prayers in Latin.

In the evening, when the flock was in the stable, a much-loved amusement after watching the sun go down was to try to count the stars. The one who counted the most stars was the winner. Those wonderful nights on the mountains, twinkling with stars and radiant with the moon, threw them almost into ecstasy. For them the stars were the lights the angels lit in the windows of heaven, the sun was our Lord's lamp, and the moon belonged to our Lady. Jacinta would say: "Our Lady's lamp pleases me more than our Lord's. It does not burn and blind me."

THREE LITTLE FACES

How can we represent the little seers of Fàtima at the moment their wonderful destiny began?

It must be remarked that all three already showed the germ of artistic and poetic, sensitive and profoundly religious souls. From their education and the constant sight of the Creator's works, they had gained the facility of mounting up to God, a facility much increased by the graces brought from heaven by the angel who visited them.

But we must not conclude that in everything they were perfect little saints. They were children of the earth, children like the others, with their own characters, their faults and little passions. They were like all the other village children. They were real little mountaineers. Their manners lacked the refinement of those of city children. But they were frank, simple, and unaffected. Tanned by the sun and the breeze, their complexions told of sturdy health.

Lucy, the true leader of the three, was just ten at this time. She was of medium height, stout, sturdy, and strong. Her sunburned face, shadowy eyes under thick-set eyebrows, and heavy lips about a wide mouth, might have deceived anyone about her rare intelligence and largeness of heart. Her hair, parted in the middle, was covered by a kerchief or *mantilla* reaching to the waist. A skirt of heavy flannel with large pleats came down to the ankles, showing only the thick, ironbound shoes.

She was not very sentimental, since she reproached her cousin for being touchy and sulky; yet she was kindhearted and could win the hearts of others, since Francis and Jacinta could not live without her. Her principal virtue was frankness. This she had gained from the example and lessons of her mother. But she had other qualities, too: obedience, humility, thoughtfulness, and a decided inclination to silence.

Francis was only nine, but already as tall as Lucy. Of the three, he seemed to have the strongest constitution. His very regular features and oval face gave him a rather dreamy expression. His hair might be called auburn; his eyes were light brown, with a kindly expression. He was even more thoughtful, silent, and discreet than his cousin. He was perfectly obedient to his father and mother, deeply devoted to his little sister, and just as pious as she, for he prayed as fervently. With his vivid imagination and bright intellect, he would certainly have made great progress at school, if he could have remained there long enough.

If anyone had to choose, though, between those three little faces, he would doubtless have found Jacinta's the most interesting.

This "little flower" of the Portuguese mountains was only seven years old. Of medium height and sturdy, she never had a serious illness. Her complexion was dark, her features very regular, her eyes deep yet singularly quick. Intelligent and lively, she was talented beyond her age. Her kind heart, her sweetness and habitual gentleness made her most amiable and affectionate.

She loved each one of her lambs. She would caress and kiss each one and press it to her heart. In the evening she carried the smallest in her arms, to save it from fatigue. One day, when she was walking home like that, in the middle of the flock with a lambkin in her arms, Francis asked her: "Jacinta, what are you doing in the middle of the sheep?"

"I am doing like our Lord. In the picture I have, Jesus is walking just so in the middle of the flock, with a little lamb in His arms."

This exquisite sensitiveness predisposed Jacinta, even more than her companions, to enjoy the celestial beauty of the Lady who was to enter so deeply into their life and to steal it away from the earth.

SECRETS FROM THE ANGELS

The Queen of Angels, we know, wished to be preceded by a messenger from the heavenly courts.

Francis and Jacinta kept the angel's visits perfectly secret, till the very hour of their death. Twenty-five years later, Sister Lucy tells about them, but with fewer details than she used in telling about those of the Blessed Virgin. Despite her extraordinarily good memory, she never could give the precise dates of the three angelic apparitions which she mentions.

It is certain, besides, that they were not the only visits of this kind; when reasons of discretion will allow it, other details may yet be known.

The providential purpose of these visits seems easy enough to guess. Was it not necessary to prepare the souls and hearts of the young shepherds for their role of confidants and messengers of Mary?

When God wished to save France by means of Joan of Arc, he sent the Archangel Michael to the little shepherdess of Lorraine, during four years, to prepare her mind and heart for her mission. In the same way, it would seem, on deciding to save our modern world by the help of three little shepherds of Aljustrel, God sent them a divine messenger to raise their souls to the height of their sublime destiny.

This angel taught them the art of praying with fervor and for those who do not pray, and of making reparation for those who have neither faith nor love. He taught them also to labor, by prayer and sacrifice, for the conversion of sinners. These are truly the interests of the Immaculate Heart of Mary, and they constitute the message of the Lady of the Cova da Iria.

As for the mystical Communion of the Cabeço, it was probably intended to increase charity in the hearts of these little lovers of Jesus. The symbolism, too, in the younger ones receiving the Precious Blood, while Lucy received the Sacred Host — did not this signify what was clearly manifested by Mary at the second apparition, namely, the difference of their earthly destinies? The Precious Blood for those who were to die victims of love, the Bread of Life for the one who was to live and suffer here below.

Were the children docile to the heavenly messenger? Their discretion is absolute on this point. In fact, it is probable that certain traits of their life (sacrifices, acts of virtue), as told in Sister Lucy's memoirs (notes), belong to this period which preceded Mary's apparitions. There is no way for us to learn of it in her accounts, in which she imposes on herself the utmost secrecy about the angel's visits. In any case, the docility which the little shepherds showed in obeying the advice of our Lady allows us to suppose a like zeal in complying with the wishes of the angel.

Knowing these facts, we shall not be surprised to see the little ones, at their first meeting with the Lady of the Cova da Iria, finding it quite natural that she should ask them for a total sacrifice and for an offering of themselves as victims of love with such generosity and enthusiasm. The divine light had made them understand, even at the second visit of the angel, the redeeming value of sacrifice, and they had already enjoyed its bitter sweetness.

Exteriorly, in the eyes of other people, their lives seemed to be the same after these meetings. Alone, in their long solitary days, they could fervently recall these delightful memories, without any one suspecting their heavenly conversations. At least, no one at home seems to have suspected these supernatural events.

Later, after the "sign of God," Olimpia was asked if her two little ones were better after having seen the Blessed Virgin. She answered that they had been as good and pious before as they were then. The mother, though most loving, had not noticed the wondrous ascensions of those secret little souls.

For its psychological interest, notice a remark made by Lucy. When the angel was at their side, the children seemed to be without self-will, or rather, with their will raised up by a supernatural force which enveloped them and drew them to imitating the angel in all his gestures and his fervor. When the angel was gone, a sort of exhaustion or physical prostration followed; they had acted as if impelled by another agent. But they felt a very great interior peace and happiness; their souls were completely centered in God.

Sister Lucy adds to this: "I do not know why our Lady's apparitions produced quite different results. It was the same interior joy, the same peace, the same felicity; but, in place of that physical fatigue, there was a certain 'expansive' vivacity; in place of that annihilation in the divine presence, an exaltation of happiness; in place of that desire for silence, a certain communicative enthusiasm."

16

DURING THE APPARITIONS

AT MARY'S SCHOOL

No one on earth will ever know the whole content of those marvelous conversations of the Lady at the evergreen oak with the shepherds of Aljustrel. For, even after the latest revelations of Sister Lucy, we probably do not yet know it all. What has been said of them, however, shows that Mary was for them an incomparable mistress of life, and that, on the other hand, they showed themselves to be her disciples, docile, fervent, and full of love.

In full possession of their love, she could obtain from them all that was possible from children of that age. You have noticed from the account of the six apparitions, that Lucy, Francis, and Jacinta made great progress in virtue from the moment they were trusted by the Lady from heaven. She knew she could count on her little disciples since, beginning with the first visit, she proposed and obtained from them total abandonment to the will of God.

It is not enough to promise. One must be faithful.

The very next day after the apparition, when they had reached the pasture, Jacinta seated herself, pensively, on a rock.

"Jacinta, come and play!"

"Today I'm not going to play!"

"Why?"

"Because I'm thinking of what the Lady told us. We must say our beads and make sacrifices. Now, when we say the beads, we shall say the *Ave Maria* all through. But, for the sacrifices, how shall we make them?"

That was an embarrassing question for their knowledge of asceticism. No one could give an answer. It was Francis who spoke first. "Let us give our food to the sheep — no *goûter!* What a pretty sacrifice!" *Goûter* was the light lunch they enjoyed between three and four o'clock.

No sooner said than done. Jacinta gave the food to the sheep. They did it every day, after that.

But the sheep, in their turn, had to make a sacrifice. One day on the road, they met the children of two very poor families of La Moita village who had been sent out to beg. Immediately Jacinta had an idea. "Let us give our lunch to those little ones!" And she hurried to bring it to them.

Pleased with this unexpected gift, the little beggars watched again for their benefactors. It became habitual to meet them at a certain place. And thus the fast days followed one another almost without interruption.

During the first hours, the three were happy for having made a sacrifice for sinners. But, toward evening, they felt their hunger and tried to satisfy it with blackberries, kernels, the roots of certain herbs, and even acorns.

The three little seers practiced every form of mortification. They seemed to have excelled in contradicting natural greediness — a thing so difficult for children of that age. When summer came, they had occasion to practice this mortification by denying themselves some very tempting fruit.

They were playing one day near the well, when Olimpia brought them some beautiful bunches of grapes, picked for them from a near-by vine arbor. They accepted them joyfully. But as soon as her mother was gone, Jacinta ran to bring them to some children playing in the street. There she met the little beggars from La Moita who, needless to say, were more than delighted at her liberality.

Another time, they had been invited to serve themselves from a basket of beautiful, fresh figs, famous for their delicacy. Jacinta rushed up to take one and then, suddenly pausing, said: "Wait! We have made no sacrifice for sinners today. Let us make this one." And, joining her hands, in the name of the three she made her offering to God.

Thus, by sacrifice, the souls of those three little friends were raised and purified. It is probable that at each apparition of their celestial Mistress they told her of their efforts to respond to her desires and that she encouraged them and guided them.

It was Mary who taught them to offer their sacrifices by saying: "O my Jesus, it is for love of You, for the conversion of sinners, and in reparation for all that offends the Immaculate Heart of Mary." This took place, remember, at the third apparition.

Along with sacrifices, she had recommended prayer, and especially the prayer of the rosary. That very first evening, Jacinta asked her mother to say the beads with her. The little seers felt obliged, not only to say the rosary themselves, but to recommend its recital at home, and even "to spread it everywhere throughout the whole world." Such was the deposition made by Mrs. Marto at the Canonical Process.

Francis and Jacinta managed the daily recital of the beads at home. For themselves, they never failed to say them, even several times a day.

The Queen of Heaven was pleased with the generosity of her little disciples and, after three months, found them capable of suffering even greater sacrifices and of bearing even a kind of little martyrdom.

THE TINSMITH'S HATRED

After the third apparition, the anticlerical mayor of Villa Nova de Ourém, Arthur d'Oliveira Santos, had determined to stop the fourth. He was much feared by the townspeople — they trembled at the thought of being called to his office. How frightened the little seers and their parents must have been when all of them received the order to present themselves before the mayor, on Saturday, August 11, the very next morning!

Mr. Marto refused to bring his children that far. They were too young to answer before a tribunal. He would go alone. But Mr. Santos went, bringing his daughter along. "She will answer for herself. I know nothing about these things. If she tells lies, let her bear the punishment."

When she parted from her cousins, Lucy kissed them affectionately. She was really frightened, and thought she might never see them again. Jacinta said: "If they want to kill you, tell them that Francis and I are just like you and that we want to die, too. We shall go to the garden behind the well, and we shall pray very hard for you."

The mayor blamed Manuel Pedro for not having obeyed punctually. Then he questioned Lucy lengthily in the presence of her father, her uncle, and some other gentlemen whom she did not know. He insisted especially upon her telling the secret, since he was sure it was the key to the mystery.

In this he failed utterly. He had to send her away, threatening that he would gain his point in the end, even if he had to kill the three guilty ones.

"When I reached home that evening," Sister Lucy recalls, "I ran straight to the garden. There I found my cousins, kneeling, their faces in their hands, their foreheads leaning against the ledge of the well, weeping bitterly. They were astonished to see me.

" 'Is that you? Your sister came to get water and she told us they had killed you. We cried and cried and we prayed for you.' "

Jacinta kissed her and said: "You see, we should never be afraid of anything. That Lady always protects us, and she loves us so!"

That little comedy was only the beginning. The thirteenth of August was drawing near, and the mayor was determined to apply the law forbidding religious celebrations outside of church. It would be easier to arrest three small children than a crowd. He tried to do it without running any risk.

The crowd had already got hold of Lucy on the morning of the thirteenth, when someone came to tell her that the mayor was waiting for her at the Marto house. There he was questioning the younger children, as he had questioned her. But he was no more successful with them. The two would neither tell the secret nor promise not to go to the Cova da Iria.

Then the official put on an amiable look, and said: "I am like Thomas; I want to see to believe." He proposed to take the children in his carriage to the Cova da Iria. Both the children and their parents refused.

Then he went away, telling the children to go to the pastor's house, because he wanted to question them before him. They went, accompanied by Mr. Marto.

At the priest's house, the magistrate pretended to talk to the children in a friendly way, standing on the little balcony where the townspeople could see him. Then he invited the children to get into his carriage and go to the Cova.

But they were no sooner on the road, than the carriage turned right instead of left and went rapidly in the direction of Ourém. The little ones cried out that they were going in the opposite direction. And the mayor said affably: "I know, but we are going first to Ourém, to the pastor's. He, too, wants to speak to you. After that, I'll drive you to the Cova in my car. We'll be there in time!"

Pleased at the prospect of a drive in an automobile, the children were quiet then; but, when they got to Ourém, they insisted on being brought to the pastor at once. They were told, however, that now they had to eat first. By this time the hour of the apparition had passed and the children were very unhappy at having missed their appointment, but the mayor was delighted. He had gained his first point.

After the meal, the three cousins thought they would be brought home. But the official insisted again that they should tell him the secret the Lady had confided to them. They persistently refused. He told them they were arrested and would come out of prison only when they consented to obey.

He shut them up in a room until the next day. In the morning an old woman came in and tried to persuade them to reveal their secret, but in vain. Then they were brought to the city hall and submitted to a close interrogation. First by insidious questions, then by threats, and finally by the temptation of gold pieces, their persecutors tried to make them talk.

The children told quite frankly all that happened to them, but they would not reveal the secret, because the Lady told them they were not to tell anyone.

About noon, they were brought back to the mayor's, where they took a little meal prepared for them by his wife, who seemed really to pity them.

In the afternoon, the martyrdom began again. They were shut
up in the public prison, whence they were told they would be
taken out to be burned alive, unless they told the secret. The other
prisoners received them well, but Jacinta drew back from the group
and went to the window. She was crying. Lucy went to console her
and asked: "Why are you crying?"

"Because we are going to die without kissing our parents. Neither
yours nor mine have come to see us. They have forgotten us. I
wish I could at least see Mamma!"

Francis found the only word that would console her: "Don't cry
any more, Jacinta. Let us offer this sacrifice for sinners." And joining
his hands, and raising his eyes to heaven, he made the offering: "O
my Jesus, it is for love of You and for the conversion of sinners —"

Jacinta joined her little hands and had the strength to add:
" — and also for the Holy Father and in reparation for what offends
the Immaculate Heart of Mary."

The other prisoners were moved by this touching scene and tried
to console them. "Why don't you tell the secret to the mayor? It's
not so terribly important."

"Oh, no!" quickly answered Jacinta. "We prefer to die!"

Then, the three captives remembered that they had not yet said
their beads for sinners. Taking a medal from her neck, Jacinta asked
a prisoner to hang it on a nail in the wall. The man obeyed, and
there the three children, on their knees, said the rosary most fervently. The other prisoners knelt down too and answered the
prayers, as best they knew how. Wonderful power of example and
of simple innocence!

Toward evening, they were brought back to the town hall where
the official tormented them by an even closer questioning, mingled
with promises and threats. Seeing them immovable, he resorted to
a final trick.

Rising suddenly, and with anger, he exclaimed: "If you won't
obey willingly, you'll obey by force!"

Then he turned to a subaltern and ordered him to prepare a large
vessel of boiling oil and to fry the obstinate children in it. In the
meantime he locked them up in another room.

A moment of real anxiety followed for the poor little victims. The door opened again, and the mayor appeared once more and called little Jacinta by name. "If you don't speak, you'll be burned first. Come here!"

The little girl (remember, she was barely seven) did not cry this time; firm in her resolution not to betray the Lady's orders, she followed the man, Sister Lucy tells, "without saying good-by to us." Again, she was questioned, caressed, threatened, and finally shut up in another room.

In the meantime, Francis was awaiting his turn with absolute tranquillity. "If they kill us, as they say, we shall be in heaven very soon. What happiness! I don't mind dying at all." And, after a moment's silence: "Let us say an *Ave Maria* for Jacinta. God help her not to be afraid!" And removing his cap, he joined his hands and prayed.

Then the mayor called Francis and told him that his sister was already fried and that the same fate awaited him if he did not reveal the secret. He refused and showed himself no less firm than Jacinta. Seizing him violently, the mayor shut him up with Jacinta.

It was Lucy's turn, and the same scene was reproduced. Today, when she is asked how she felt, Sister Lucy answers: "I was convinced that that man was speaking the truth, and that henceforth all was finished for me on earth. But I was not afraid and I recommended myself to the Blessed Virgin."

But the mayor was only playing his little game. Lucy found her cousins safe and sound, but afraid. The next day was the great Feast of the Assumption. After spending the night at the mayor's, the children were brought back to the town hall. There they were submitted to another questioning.

Gaining nothing, the mayor at last resolved to bring them back to Fàtima. He arrived there during High Mass. He brought the children to the priest's house, and sat with them on the veranda. When the people came out of church, a man said to Mr. Marto: "Look at your children on the priest's porch, with the mayor." Manuel Pedro joined them, and the Tinsmith looked quite innocent. "All has gone well. The children may go back to the Cova da Iria" —

he had just told them he would have them arrested if they returned there.

Just then a group of young men armed with sticks came toward them with a not very encouraging air. The Tinsmith had noticed them, so he invited Manuel Pedro to go along for a friendly glass at the café. To avoid possible violence, Mr. Marto accepted; and when the young men saw the victims' father and their persecutor on such good terms, they thought it all was settled and went away without further investigation.

During this time, having kissed their parents, Lucy, Francis, and Jacinta ran off to the Cova to thank our Lady. Jacinta's parents had sent one of their older sons to make inquiries at the mayor's office during these two terrible days. But Maria Rosa had showed herself almost harsh about it. She had said to the one who told her of her daughter's kidnaping:

"That's good. If it's lies she's telling, she'll have what she deserves. If it's true, the Blessed Virgin will defend her."

The Blessed Virgin had indeed defended Lucy. And she came from heaven, four days later, to console her little friends.

THIRST FOR SUFFERING

The Lady of Light confided to the children, when she spoke to them at the Valinhos, that many souls go to hell because there are none to make sacrifices for them. This thought was often repeated in their secret conversations and exercised a decisive influence upon their moral life. It redoubled, if possible, their will to offer themselves as victims for poor sinners, that these might not fall into the terrible flames they had seen on the thirteenth of July. They sought to mortify themselves by thirst as well as hunger.

One especially hot day in August, the little shepherds had met their friends from La Moita and given them their usual alms. In the afternoon, they could no longer resist their thirst. There was a group of cottages quite near, so Lucy went to knock at a door and ask for water. A little old woman answered her, gave her a pitcher of water, and added a piece of bread. The bread was shared among the three, and Lucy handed the pitcher to Francis.

"I don't want to drink."

"Why?"

"I want to suffer for the conversion of sinners."

"You drink, Jacinta!"

"I, too, want to do penance."

Then Lucy poured the pitcher of water into a hollow stone for the sheep. From time to time, they promised to spend a novena, or even a month, without drinking, except at the home meals. They also sought directly to mortify their bodies.

Once Jacinta accidentally pricked herself with nettles. She took a handful and offered them to the others. "See! See! Here is something we can mortify ourselves with!" And they set about beating their legs with the nettles — a penance they repeated whenever they found those weeds.

Between the fourth and the fifth apparitions, they found a rope on the road. As they walked along, Lucy kept twisting it around her wrist. She noticed that the cord chafed her skin. "Do you know that hurts? We might tie it around our waist and offer that sacrifice to God." The idea was accepted. They had no knife to cut it, but they found a sharp pebble with which to knock the rope against a rock, and soon each one had a penitential girdle.

The rope was heavy and rough, or else it was tied too tightly; sometimes it hurt horribly. Jacinta sometimes cried over it. If Lucy advised her to take it off, she answered: "No! I must suffer in reparation for sins and for the conversion of sinners."

At first, they wore this hard belt night and day. But at her next visit, on the thirteenth of September, the Lady of the Cova said to them, with maternal kindness: "Our Lord is pleased with your sacrifices, but He does not wish you to wear that cord in bed. Wear it only during the day." The children obeyed. They persevered in that penance because it pleased Jesus and Mary.

How many other similar sacrifices did these generous children make? God only knows the number. The difficulty was to keep them secret and especially to hide them from their parents, for they had spoken to no one of the promise they had made to our Lady nor of what they did to be faithful to it.

It was only twenty years later, and at the pressing invitation of the bishop of Leiria, who wished to know the merits of little Jacinta, that Lucy, now Sister Mary of the Dolors, revealed the sacrifices related above.

The marks of a divine work are always humility and discretion, which make this thirst of suffering for souls all the more touching. Happy children, who in a few days so perfectly understood the mystery of the cross, the most difficult and sublime element of the science that makes saints.

THE PARENTS' COLDNESS

One thing they found particularly hard was the lack of understanding on the part of their own people. The Marto parents did not torment Francis and Jacinta, but their brothers and sisters did plenty of teasing.

At the Santos, though, Lucy was isolated, abandoned, if not cast aside. This was a cruel torture for her affectionate heart, and one of the principal reasons for her discouragement after the third apparition. She was accused of being a liar, a pretended saint, and of causing the loss of the crops at the Cova da Iria.

Antonio did have more there than the rocky land around the evergreen oaks (or holm trees); in the lower part was a sufficiently fertile field which produced a good crop of potatoes every year. The rest of the land was a fair pasture for the cattle. But with the crowds that came to the place for the visions, there could be no crops at all. Everything was trampled down and crushed by the people, their horses and carriages.

Maria Rosa lamented this loss and would sometimes say to Lucy: "You, girl! Some day when you're hungry, you can go and ask your Lady for something to eat!"

The other daughters would exaggerate what their mother said, as if they wished to humiliate this "pretended Bernadette."

The poor little girl reached the point of asking herself if she had the right to take a bite of bread at table.

They counted the loss of time, too. Somebody was always called upon to run after Lucy, because people wanted to see her. About mid-September they had to sell the flock, and so deprive the family of the profit it used to bring them.

However, the Santos family must not be accused of avarice. They proved their generosity, first by never claiming a cent of the money left by the pilgrims on their land, and then by selling this property at a very low price. The bishop himself recognized this act publicly. It seems that the whole family wanted to find out for sure whether Lucy deserved the visits of the Blessed Virgin.

There was only one recourse for her then: to remember her promise to the Lady to suffer all things for sinners.

After the fourth apparition (August 19) and especially after the "sign of God" (October 13), these marks of hostility calmed down. Antonio, who pretended not to bother about these "women's stories," tolerated his daughter's persecution even less. They teased her too much. "Leave her alone," he would say. "We don't know the truth of what she says, but we can't prove it to be false."

Olimpia and Manuel Pedro were too certain of their children's loyalty to treat them like liars. They did not understand, but they accepted the mystery. They certainly would not allow their two little ones to be injured or mistreated, as did Lucy's parents. Desiring suffering as they did, Francis and Jacinta even regretted their privileged situation. They thus lost an occasion of suffering for our Lord.

WHAT THE CLERGY THOUGHT

One cross that all three bore equally was the indifference, not to say coldness, of the father of their souls, the pastor of Fàtima. Of course, he was always just, paternal, and correct; but he could not admit the truth of the visions.

Doubtless, he was badly impressed by the reticence in the children's story and by the famous secret. He believed the stories of those who complained that his three little parishioners were not amiable to those who wanted to question them. Father Ferreira would have wished them to answer everyone, and especially his fellow priests, with invariable patience. Moreover, there was no end to the worries these events caused him. No one appreciated his "neutrality." Some blamed him for not putting a stop to this "comedy"; others accused him of being in league with the freethinkers.

This second accusation took a serious turn among the people when they saw the mayor of Ourém leave the priest's house to arrest the children. They suspected the priest of complicity with the Tinsmith and, had it not been for the prodigies at the Cova da Iria, they would have made it difficult for both of them. The calumnious rumor spread so fast, that Father Ferreira thought it best to write an explanatory letter to the Lisbon newspaper, *A Ordem,* on August 15, 1917. He said his life had been in danger on the thirteenth. He explained why he did not go to the Cova da Iria with the crowd on the thirteenth of each month. The patriarchate of Lisbon had asked the clergy to remain neutral in this affair. Besides, if the apparitions were supernatural, his presence was not necessary; if they were not, by assisting he would furnish arguments to the enemies of religion.

The good priest almost blamed his little parishioners for all these difficulties. And when he saw thousands of people on a desert prairie, going to the Cova, he could not help thinking they would have done better to stop at his church and pray to God. His church was badly in need of repairs, and people were casting useful money at the foot of a tree! Since that time, however, the church of Fàtima has been suitably cared for and even enlarged.

If, despite his "neutrality," Father Manuel Ferreira never did anything that might have positively humiliated the little seers, the same could not be said of some of his fellow priests. There were priests among the curious people who pestered the little ones with questions. Some of them asked indiscreet questions or ridiculed the answers given them. Respecting the clergy as they did, the children were very much hurt by this.

Still, many priests encouraged them and helped them with advice. The saintly and popular Father Cruz, who had admitted Lucy to First Communion three years before, returned to Fàtima to meet the little seers and to clear up the whole story of the apparitions. Radiating virtue and kindliness, he quickly won the confidence of the children who opened their hearts to him with absolute frankness. He himself was convinced of their perfect sincerity.

After a long conversation with them, he asked Lucy and Jacinta to bring him to the place of the apparitions. He went, mounted on a donkey so small that his feet touched the ground, while one little girl walked on his right, the other on his left. Together they spoke of the Blessed Virgin and recited the rosary. Then Father Cruz taught them pious ejaculations that might help to keep their hearts raised to God during the day.

Still another priest advised them to be very grateful to God for all the graces they had received. From that day on they formed the habit of saying from time to time: "My God, I love You in return for all the graces You have granted me."

Jacinta loved to say this prayer continuously, for she said: "I love our Lord and the Blessed Virgin so much that I never get tired of repeating it."

After the third apparition, two priests spoke to them with much love and conviction about the pope and his trials and responsibilities. From that moment they added "and for the Holy Father" to their formula of offering and, after every rosary, three Hail Marys for his intentions.

But he who oftenest encouraged the little shepherds of Aljustrel in their mission as seers and victims was Father Faustino Jacinto Ferreira, pastor of Olival and archpriest of Ourém. Pious, zealous, learned, and very popular, he conceived a true friendship for Lucy, Francis, and Jacinta from their first meeting. He made a point of introducing them to the spiritual life and of teaching them the practice of penance.

A number of times he took Lucy home with him to teach her, encourage her, and give her wise advice. Sister Mary of the Dolors retained a most profound gratitude for her first teacher in the spiritual life.

Later, he declared himself a believer in the truth of the apparitions, and the bishop of Leiria named him a member of the Canonical Commission of Inquiry.

17

FROM THE APPARITIONS TO THE DEATH OF FRANCIS

THE TRIAL OF THE INQUISITIONS

As the apparitions were repeated, the crowds grew more numerous at the Cova, and Antonio's land became a kind of sanctuary, without an altar and without a priest. All these people, or nearly all of them, wished to see the children and to speak to them. On the day of the great miracle, especially, the children were the prey of the curious. Their parents had to draw them away from the crowd to make them eat and rest. Toward midnight, Lucy was so worn out that she let herself fall to the floor in a dead sleep. People spent the whole night in the country in order to question her the next day. The same situation was to continue for the children without a letup. More than ever, they were to be questioned by correspondents, doctors, ecclesiastics, and curiosity seekers. Some were believers, some freethinkers, some atheists, some simply curious. "Those who come are so numerous," Maria Rosa told the pastor of Fàtima on the twenty-fifth of October, "that it's a great miracle the children are not yet sick."

For the children themselves all this was a real torture, which they usually offered to our Lord, but which they sometimes could not bear and always tried to avoid. They were tired of repeating the same things, and afraid of revealing the secret confided by the vision, even of letting their penances and sacrifices be known. So there was a kind of rivalry to find the best means of escaping indiscreet people without failing in charity or in truth.

112

One day, while on a bad road connecting Aljustrel with the main thoroughfare, they saw a car stopping at the crossroad and a group of well-dressed ladies and gentlemen leaving it. There was no doubt at all about whom these people were seeking. "If we run away," the children argued, "we'll be noticed. Let's go toward them."

The strangers approached and stopped them. "Do you know the little shepherds who see the Blessed Virgin?"

"Yes, we know them."

"Could you tell us where they live?"

"Take that crossroad. Over there, you turn to the left —" And Lucy minutely described her house and that of her cousins.

The travelers left, thanking the children who, gay as larks, went to hide in the fields.

Another time, Francis, walking ahead, saw a group of fine ladies with hats as big as sieves coming toward them. "Let's climb up this fig tree," he said. "With those things on their heads, they won't see us."

The ladies did, in fact, pass under the trees and under the children without perceiving them. Once they were out of sight, the three escaped into a field of corn.

Often they would vanish for hours and hours without anyone being able to find them. Where were they? It was never known. But, in her recollections of Jacinta, Sister Lucy reveals it. They were "behind the well" of the Santos garden, disappearing at any given moment behind the hedges and the shrubbery. Sometimes they went to that grottolike place called the "Cabeço hole," where they received the first visit of the angel of Portugal.

There, as "behind the well," they prayed for the intentions of the Lady and talked of the things she had confided to them. There they were in peace and could recite the "Angel's prayers," doing this sometimes for hours at a time until they fell down from fatigue. There, too, they could perform their little penances without curious witnesses.

If they thus hid themselves it was not because they wished to avoid all inquiry. They had told about the apparitions hundreds of times; their accounts had been taken down in shorthand; they had frequently been photographed. Was it any use, they wondered, always to repeat the same thing?

And then so many people evidently sought to embarrass them with tricky questions. They were mere children, and people tried to make them say foolish things. Surely they had a right to defend themselves.

On the other hand, Dr. Formigâo and other serious men have often borne witness to the politeness of the little seers, when they were properly questioned for a good reason.

One who was an eyewitness of the phenomena of the fifth apparition, says: "As soon as we arrived at Fàtima, my friend and I went to the children's homes to photograph them and to question them. That meeting was the most charming of my trip. Their angelic simplicity was proof conclusive that they were not lying."

We must not forget, too, that these questionings often put before them a rather troublesome case of conscience. They had resolved to say nothing of their promise to the Lady to sacrifice themselves for sinners, nor of the penances they performed in consequence of this promise. They did not wish to make a display of themselves as victims and martyrs. Would they not have lost the merit of their actions? And would not their parents have interfered with them?

But were they telling lies when inquisitive people asked them if the Blessed Virgin had said anything else, and they said, "No"? On this point, in particular, the directions of the pastor of Olival were most helpful to them.

SCHOLARS

At the second apparition, the Lady had advised Lucy to learn to read. When she was asked why she did not go to school, she could answer nothing. But after her parents had sold the flock, there was nothing to prevent the realization of Mary's wish. Her cousins, also freed from the care of the sheep, accompanied her to the village school.

The three latecomers were a curiosity to the others. But they were intelligent and hard working and made rapid progress. The two younger ones were especially anxious to learn their catechism in order to make their First Communion.

Francis knew that for him the science of this world was of no use. In consequence, he often spent even his schooltime at the foot of the altar in the village church.

In Fàtima they went together to salute Jesus, hidden in the tabernacle. Francis would sometimes say to Lucy: "It is necessary for you to go to school. But I'll remain here. Very soon I'll be going to heaven. Is it any use for me to study? After class, you'll stop and take me home."

At recess, Lucy and Jacinta left their schoolmates playing and joined him before the Blessed Sacrament.

"People seem to guess my thoughts," Jacinta would say. "As soon as I go into the church, other people come in too. I would so love to be alone with Jesus. But they never leave us alone."

On one occasion people from a neighboring village had come to ask the little prophets to pray for some sinner who was causing disgrace and unhappiness in their family.

"We shall pray for him," they said, "and offer sacrifices that he may be converted and not go to hell, the poor man!"

After class, they found Francis in a corner of the church, near the altar where the Blessed Sacrament was kept.

When school was over, Jacinta, Francis, and Lucy sometimes went to the Cova da Iria, where they thought there would be fewer people at that hour in the evening. But even then they sometimes found pilgrims and had to listen to their questions and petitions, or even receive their compliments and be kissed by them — a terrible trial for their humility.

But, despite these annoyances, the three little friends found some privacy behind Lucy's well or in the Cabeço recess. There, far from everyone and everything, they prayed together and encouraged one another to suffer. They lived the delightful hours of the apparitions over again. They exchanged thoughts on the promises they had made to the Lady and on the secret she had entrusted to them. For the rest, the three scholars were so careful that nothing seemed to distinguish them from their schoolmates in the village.

They were truly "seers" but they had not ceased to be children. They talked, laughed, and sang as before. They were determined to be just like the others and not to draw attention to themselves. Humility had no more secrets for them than mortification.

When they were alone they talked much — but if anyone drew near they became silent, or else quietly fell in with the conversation of the newcomers.

Someone asked Olimpia: "Have you noticed any great change in your children?"

"Nothing extraordinary. They are just as good and as affectionate as they were before," answered the mother, with tears in her eyes.

Yes, they were like the others in all things. But they kept an important secret to themselves, and their eyes were ever open upon the awesome destiny awaiting them.

EXTRAORDINARY FAVORS

Our Lady did not forget her little messengers. She had promised that if they were docile she would hear their prayers. She was doubtless satisfied with their obedience, since, now and then, she granted them some very choice favor.

They never refused prayers to those who asked for them. And it sometimes happened that the Blessed Virgin granted them visibly.

One poor woman threw herself on her knees before Jacinta, crying and begging her to obtain from our Lady her cure of a painful infirmity. Jacinta took the poor woman by the hands and tried to raise her. Proving too weak for this, the child knelt down beside her and prayed for her. Soon, the woman returned to give thanks to our Lady at the Cova da Iria for her cure.

Another time, it was a soldier who came, crying like a child, to recommend himself to the prayers of the little prophets. He had been called to war, and must leave his sick wife with their three young children.

"Don't cry," said Jacinta, "our Lady is so good!"

The little shepherds prayed for the soldier and added an *Ave Maria* for him to their daily beads.

At the end of a few months, the man came back with his wife

and children to thank our Lady. His prayer had been doubly granted. On the eve of the departure, he was stricken with a sudden fever, and had been sent home on an unlimited furlough. And soon his wife found herself cured "by a real miracle of our Lady's," he declared.

There was a woman in the parish who used to insult the seers whenever she met them. One day, as she stumbled out of a tavern, quite tipsy, she added blows to the usual insults.

When they had escaped from her, Jacinta said: "We must pray hard to our Lady for the conversion of that woman and make sacrifices for her. She says so many sinful things, and such terribly bad things, that if she does not confess them she will go to hell."

A few days later, the two little girls were playing tag, and happened to pass the vixen's house. Jacinta stopped suddenly and said to Lucy: "Let's stop playing! It will be a sacrifice for the conversion of sinners."

And, without thinking that she might be seen, she joined her hands, raised her eyes to heaven, and recited the formula of offering. The poor woman was watching the children through a little window in her house. She was so much won by Jacinta's prayer that she stopped insulting them, asked them to pray for her, and became a fervent petitioner at the Cova da Iria.

Sister Lucy also tells about the Mrs. Emilia from la Soutaria, a village of the parish of Olival, who came to take her and Jacinta to the pastor of Olival for the first time.

It was night when they arrived at la Soutaria, and so it was decided that the children should sleep there. But many people came to see them, simply out of curiosity. Among them was a pious lady who used to gather a group of good souls about her every day to say the rosary. She asked that the children might come to say the beads with her friends; and they consented, but the crowd followed them.

On the way the two little girls were stopped by a young lady in tears who begged them to come into her home to see her father and pray for his cure. He had been afflicted for three years with an intolerable, continual hiccough. Jacinta offered to remain with the

man and to pray for him. Three days later, when they were leaving
for Aljustrel, the young girl and her father stopped the children to
thank them. The man was cured.

Here is an even more curious fact. An aunt of Lucy's, living at
Fàtima, had a son who had left home and was never heard from.
This woman came to see her niece and ask her to pray for the
prodigal. Lucy was away, so the request was presented to Jacinta.

After a few days, the young man returned and begged his
parents' pardon. On his way home at night, he said, he had got lost
in the mountains and woods, and a violent storm blew up. Thoroughly frightened, he had fallen on his knees imploring God's
mercy, when suddenly he saw his cousin Jacinta beside him. She
had given him her hand and led him to the road, then left him,
after pointing in the direction he was to go.

When explanations were asked of Jacinta, she answered: "I don't
know where those forests or those mountains are. But I prayed
hard to our Lady for him, because of Aunt Victoria's sorrow."

"How all that happened," said Sister Lucy, "I don't know, but
God knows."

SOULS OF THE SEERS

It is hard to realize the peace that possessed the souls of these
children at the thought of the Lady of the Cova da Iria and the
way she favored them.

Where Sister Lucy is concerned, you can only try to guess it,
for in the accounts she gives she is very careful to speak as little
of herself as possible. Resolutely, ceaselessly, she puts herself aside
to speak mainly of her cousins. We know nothing of what concerns
herself, of how Mary's words struck her, of the impression such
or such a part of our Lady's message made upon her. What did
she particularly love to speak about with her two little confidants?
Since she was to remain in this world, the only keeper of the secret
till the time marked by Providence, she probably thought herself
more personally responsible for that trust. Thoughts about her
own future, about the future of her own country and of the world,
about her role in diffusing devotion to the Immaculate Heart of

Mary; previsions concerning the actual war, perhaps concerning other events still unknown to us — such reflections may have filled her mind, inspired her prayers, and entered into her conversations with her little cousins.

It can easily be seen that Jacinta's delicate heart had retained especially the vision of the sufferings of the damned. Since the terrible apparition of hell (July 13), she could not detach her thought from it. That very evening, she had asked Lucy for explanations on the eternity of hell which so vividly impressed her.

"Even after many years, hell will not be over? And those people burning in it will never die . . . they will not become ashes? And if Christians pray a great deal for those poor people, the good God will not take them out of there? Not even if they make many sacrifices?"

"No, not if they died in the state of mortal sin. But we can pray and offer sacrifices for sinners that they may be converted, as our Lady told us."

"Poor unhappy people! Then we shall pray much and do penance for the conversion of sinners."

Sometimes, she would be seated very thoughtfully, repeating: "Hell! . . . Hell! . . . How sorry I feel for those souls who fall into it! And the people there burn like wood in the fire! We must pray very much to prevent souls from going to hell."

Then, trembling from fright and sorrow, she would kneel down, with her hands joined, and say the prayer the Lady taught them: "O my Jesus, forgive us, etc."

When there were crowds at the Cova, she would say to Lucy: "You should ask our Lady to show hell to all those people there! You would see how they would all be converted." And pensively she would add: "So many people fall into hell! So many people!"

"Don't be afraid, since you will go to heaven!"

"I know it. But, I wish all those people would come too."

Later on, if she was to show great courage during her long, cruel sickness, it was because of the thought that her sufferings converted sinners and saved them from damnation.

She also kept a deep impression of the second apparition, when the mysterious light had revealed to them the loveliness of the Immaculate Heart of Mary.

Sometimes she would say to Lucy:

"Our Lady said that her Immaculate Heart would be your refuge and your way to God. Doesn't that make you glad? I so love her Heart! It is so good!"

And she would add, with childlike simplicity: "I so love the Immaculate Heart of Mary! It is the Heart of our Mother in heaven! Don't you find it sweet to repeat often: Heart of Mary! Sweet Heart of Mary! I have so much pleasure in it! So much pleasure!"

While she gathered flowers in the country, she would sing to a tune she had improvised herself: "Sweet Heart of Mary, be my salvation! Immaculate Heart of Mary, convert sinners, save their souls from hell!"

Knowing Mary's desires concerning Communion of reparation, she would sweetly complain: "I'm so sorry not to be able to go to Communion in reparation for the sins which offend the Immaculate Heart of Mary!"

Francis was most impressed by the sweetness of the divine presence and the thought that so good a God was offended by sin.

He often left his companions and went off to pray alone, in order to concentrate better on God. He would be absorbed in the thought of that immense light in which, at the first apparition and at two others, all three of them had been plunged. He often spoke of it to his companions.

"We were like on fire in that light and yet we did not burn! How wonderful God is! He is so beautiful that we can't express it. But what a shame that He should be so sad! If only I could console Him!" To console God, who is so good yet so saddened by the sins of the world, that was his great thought.

One day he had gone aside and climbed a high rock, while Jacinta and Lucy were catching butterflies, "so as to make a sacrifice by letting them fly away!" When the little girls were tired of running and wanted to pray with him, he called them up on his promontory, where there was hardly room for all three to kneel.

"Why do you stay up there so long?" asked his sister.

"I am thinking of our Lord, who is grieved by so many sins. If only I were able to satisfy Him!" With this intention in mind, he would spend all day in prayer, without even eating.

He would say: "I was very glad to see the angel, and much more to see the Blessed Virgin; but, what I loved most was to see God in that great light the Lady put into our heart. I love our Lord so! But He is sad because of sin! Oh, if I could only console Him! No, we shall never commit another single sin!"

One day, in the fall of 1917, Lucy asked him what pleased him better, that his sacrifices should console our Lord or deliver souls from hell.

"If I were to choose, I would rather console our Lord. Didn't you notice how the Blessed Virgin became so sad last month, when she asked that 'they should no more offend our Lord, who is so much offended'? I would wish to console our Lord, and also to convert sinners so that they would not offend Him any more."

Sister Lucy also says that one day, when Jacinta did not want to go alone to stand guard at a place she pointed out, Francis offered to go in her place, "to do it for sinners." When he did not come back, she sent Jacinta for him. But Jacinta couldn't find him, so she called with all her might and then came back much distressed.

Then Lucy went in her turn. She also called and got no answer. Finally, she found him, prostrate in prayer behind a heap of stones which hid him from sight. She had to shake him to bring him back to consciousness.

"Were you praying?"

"Yes, I started out saying the angel's prayer, and since that I was busy thinking."

This little fellow of ten could absorb himself in God to the point of not hearing his name called a few yards away.

No wonder that these souls, thus united to God and so pleasing to Mary, should have been favored with extraordinary graces. There is reason to believe, in fact, that during the period from 1917–1918 the little seers received other visits from the Queen of Heaven. But, wishing to speak only of what is published with ecclesiastical approval, we shall limit ourselves to the apparitions to Francis and Jacinta during their illness.

They seem also to have had some kind of prophetic visions.

One day Jacinta had remained near the well while her brother and her cousin had gone to look for wild honey in the near-by shrubs. The two heard her call: "Lucy! Lucy! Did you see the Holy Father?"

"The Holy Father? No."

"I don't know how it happened but I saw him in a very big house, kneeling before a little table (a prie-dieu) with his face in his hands and crying. Outside, there were many people. Some were throwing stones, others were insulting him and saying bad words. Poor Holy Father!"

A few days later, when the two priests mentioned before had advised the little girls to pray for the pope, Jacinta said to her companions: "But that is the one I saw crying, and of whom the Lady spoke in the secret, isn't it? The Lady must have showed him to those two priests, too. You see, we can't be wrong, and we must pray very hard for him."

Another time, while they were saying the angel's prayer in the Cabeço grotto, Jacinta rose to her feet and called out to her cousin: "Look! Don't you see all those roads, all those paths, and those fields filled with people crying with hunger who have nothing to eat? And the Holy Father praying in a church before the Immaculate Heart of Mary? And so many people in the world praying together with him? . . ."

This vision seems to have been realized on December 8, 1942, when His Holiness Pius XII solemnly consecrated the Church and the world to the Immaculate Heart of Mary, in the Basilica of St. Peter, before an enormous crowd.

Jacinta afterward asked Lucy if she might say that she had seen the Holy Father. Her cousin dissuaded her, because by that people could guess a part of her secret.

SICKNESS AND DEATH OF FRANCIS

On December 23, 1918, Jacinta and Francis both fell sick. They were stricken with that terrible Spanish influenza which caused such ravages throughout the world. Successively, all the members of the Marto family, except the father, were laid low. Here are the names and dates of death of the victims of that dread malady: Francis, April 4, 1919; Jacinta, February 20, 1920; Florinda, 1920; Theresa, 1921. In the Santos family, only the father died, July 31, 1919.

Help came from some relations and some charitable neighbors; Manuel Pedro was general infirmarian.

No sickness could diminish the fervor in prayer and sacrifice of the brother and sister. They seemed even happy to have more occasion to suffer for sinners.

Francis was to die first. Of the three seers of Fàtima, he is the most forgotten. In the apparitions his was the most hidden role: he did not even hear the sweet Lady's voice.

But, was it necessary for him to hear, since he had so little witness to bear? To realize the beauty of the heaven that awaited him and to desire it, was it not sufficient that he should see? Anyway, Mary came for him first. Was it not because he was most worthy? He was never less faithful nor less generous than his sister and his cousin. And how fervently he prayed! He never forgot that our Lady had promised him paradise, on the condition that he said many rosaries. He forgot it even less when he was kept in bed by sickness. Even when suffering from the worst fever, he thought of his beads and said them several times a day.

During the first weeks of his illness, he could not leave his bed. "He suffered with heroic patience during the time of sickness," writes Sister Lucy, "without a moan or a complaint. He took everything his mother brought him, and I could never discover whether anything displeased him."

When Lucy came to see him, he asked her to say the beads with him. If he was too weak to say the five decades running, he was much distressed. His mother consoled him by telling him that our Lady was just as much pleased by mental prayer.

On certain days, when he could be up and felt strong enough to go out, he would climb up to the Cova da Iria. There he would renew in his mind the image of the Lady of Light, saying that his one desire was to see her again in heaven.

Good souls whom he met tried to console him by saying that he would soon be cured. But, with a look of assurance, he would invariably answer, "No."

His godmother told him one day she would make a promise to our Lady if he were cured. She wanted to promise our Lady, for the expenses of her altar, a weight of wheat equal to the child's weight. This is a favorite promise among the Portuguese.

"It's useless to think of it, godmother. I won't be cured."

Toward the end of February the little boy's sickness grew much worse. He had to go back to bed. Jacinta, who was also suffering much at the time, would come to spend long hours at his bed. If Lucy came, and they were alone, they would talk about the Lady and pray together.

One day Lucy asked her cousin: "Francis, do you suffer much?"

"Yes, very much. But I bear it for the love of Jesus and Mary." He had always worn the cord of penance around his waist. Now he was unable to wear it any longer, so he gave it to his cousin.

It was about this time that he and his sister were favored with a visit from the Blessed Virgin. Jacinta told it to Lucy.

"Our Lady came to see us. She said she would soon come to take Francis to heaven. She asked me if I were willing to convert other sinners. I told her, yes, I was willing.

"She told me I would go to another hospital, where I would suffer very much, but I must bear it all for the conversion of sinners, and in reparation for sins against the Immaculate Heart of Mary.

"I thought of our Lord and His holy Mother, of sinners and the war that is to come. So many people are to die! So many people will go to hell! There will be so many houses destroyed! So many priests killed! What sorrows! If people ceased offending God, the war would not come and souls would not go to hell. Listen, I am going to heaven. But you, that night when you will see the light our Lady spoke of, run away and come up to heaven!"

"But I don't think we can run away to heaven!" answered Francis.

"It's true, that's impossible! But don't be afraid! I'll pray a great deal for you in heaven, for the Holy Father, for Portugal, that the war may not come here, and for all priests."

Francis was growing steadily weaker. The little invalid continued to give first place to his intention of consoling Jesus and His holy Mother. He often offered them his sufferings, which were very great.

One day, he said to his cousin: "You see, I am very weak, I am going to heaven very soon."

"Well," answered Lucy, "when you are there, don't forget to pray very much for sinners, for the Holy Father, and for Jacinta and me."

Then, always preoccupied and absorbed by the vision of God, he answered with his absolute simplicity: "Yes, I shall pray! But, I think you'd better tell Jacinta these things because I'm afraid I shall not think of them when I see our Lord. I shall so want to console Him!"

Now, his condition was growing worse every day. His appetite was gone, he took scarcely any food, and his strength failed rapidly.

One morning, very early, his sister Theresa ran to get Lucy, for Francis was worse and wanted to speak to her. Lucy dressed quickly and hurried over. The little invalid sent everyone out of his room.

He must go to confession that very day to prepare himself for death. He wants his cousin to help him examine his conscience. Lucy can think of no other sin but disobeying his mother to get away from curious people. Jacinta, called in her turn, remembers two other peccadillos. Before the apparitions, he had taken ten cents from the house to buy a harmonica, and when the Aljustrel children threw stones at the Boleiros, he had thrown some too.

"That's true, and I confessed it. But I'll confess them again. Who knows if, by those sins, I have caused our Lord to be so sad? But now, even if I were not to die, I should never commit them again. I am very sorry for them." And joining his hands, he recited the prayer: "O my Jesus, forgive us our sins. . . . "

He begged Lucy to ask pardon for him, and she reassured him: "If Jesus had not pardoned you, the Blessed Virgin would not have told Jacinta the other day that she was going to take you very soon to paradise."

Lucy left him, then, to go to Mass.

"Ask the hidden Jesus that Father Pastor may give me Holy Communion!"

It was the second of April. Finding her little boy much worse, Olimpia called for the pastor. Besides, Easter was drawing near.

Francis' great fear was that the priest might not bring him Viaticum because he had not yet made his First Communion.

What a joy when Father Ferreira, after hearing his confession, promised to bring him Holy Communion the next morning!

He wanted to remain fasting and when the priest returned he asked to confess himself again, in order to receive our Lord with more respect.

He received the Sacred Host "with a great lucidity of mind and great piety," the pastor said at the Canonical Process, and seemed to be radiant with joy.

And when he was alone with Lucy and Jacinta, he told them: "I am going to heaven soon. I'll ask Jesus and the Blessed Virgin to bring you there, too, very soon."

His godmother had been his infirmarian. He asked her pardon for all the trouble he had given her.

The next morning, the fourth of April, at about six o'clock, he said to his mother:

"Mamma, look at the beautiful light near the door!"

And, after a minute: "Now, I don't see it any more!"

Then his face was brightened with an angelic smile, and without a groan, he gently expired. Born on July 11, 1908, he was not yet eleven years old.

18

SICKNESS AND DEATH OF JACINTA

"ALL THAT THEY SHALL WANT"

When Francis had spoken his farewells on the eve of his death, Jacinta entrusted him with her messages for heaven. Using a favorite Portuguese expression, she said: "Give many compliments for me to our Lord and our Lady. *Tell them I shall suffer all they want* for sinners and to make reparation to the Immaculate Heart of Mary."

"Suffer all that God wills." This was to be the program of her life. We have known Jacinta: plaintive, delicate, loving games and dances to excess. Now grace has transformed her soul. She has become patient, strong, and even hard in the face of suffering. She knows that nothing counts here below, except to save one's soul and the souls of others. This little girl of nine shows herself a heroic penitent, a victim of love, a true martyr.

And as she approached her end, her love for Jesus and Mary, her resignation, and her spirit of sacrifice gained in intensity, as if she wished to make a supreme effort, as long as there was time to merit a more beautiful crown.

She often thought of her brother Francis. "How much I long to see him!" she would say with tears. She wanted to go where he was, with Jesus whom she loved.

She would often repeat her favorite prayer: "O my Jesus, I love you!"

If Lucy came to see her, she would ask her to repeat it with her. "I love so to tell Jesus that I love Him. When I say it very often, it seems to me I have a flame in my breast, but a flame that does not burn."

Again she would say: "I love our Lord and the Blessed Virgin so much that I am never tired of telling them so."

For love of them, she patiently bore her cruel sickness. Her case of influenza had degenerated by this time into pleurisy, with other complications. Sometimes she suffered greatly, but did not show it outwardly.

"Look here, Jacinta, are you any better?"

"You know very well I'm not. How sore my side is! But I suffer it for sinners."

She also had to get rid of her little rope of penance so she gave it to Lucy. "Keep it for me. I am afraid mother might see it. If I get better, I shall ask you to return it."

This cord had three knots in it — and it was a little stained with blood. Lucy hid it carefully. Later, she burned it with Francis'.

Olimpia was grieving over her daughter's condition. "Why are you so sad?" Jacinta asked. "I'm all right."

Another day: "Don't be sad, Mamma! I'm going to heaven. There, I shall pray very much for you."

She loved Lucy's visits. When her cousin came, she would talk about the secret and the other things the Lady told them. But now Lucy spent nearly all day in school. What a penance to offer to Jesus!

Her friend tried to make up for this absence by bringing flowers, preferably some taken from about the Cabeço grotto which recalled so many memories.

"I shall never go over there again," said the little one, "nor to Valinhos, nor to the Cova da Iria! And I am so sorry!"

"But what does it matter to you? You are going to heaven, to see our Lord and our Lady!"

"That's true." And she remained quite happy.

One day, in the spring of 1919, she announced to Lucy, in a voice broken by sobs: "Our Lady appeared to me! She wants me to go to two hospitals. But it is not to be cured. I am to suffer very much. I shall die soon . . . and I shall die without having received the hidden Jesus! If only our Lady would bring Him with her when she comes for me!"

TO LOVE AND BE LOVED

About this time, a cousin gave her a picture representing a chalice and a host. She took it, kissed it tenderly, and said, as if carried away by a beautiful dream or by a distant vision — and doubtless, too, plunged in the sweet recollection of the mystic Communion at the Cabeço: "It is the hidden Jesus. I love Him so! Who will let me receive Him in church? Is there Communion in heaven? If there is, I shall go every day. If the angel came to the hospital to bring me Holy Communion a second time, how happy I should be!"

When Lucy came back from church after Communion, Jacinta would make her come quite close so that she might feel the divine presence. She would sometimes say: "I don't know how it is. I feel our Lord within me. I understand what He says to me without seeing Him or hearing Him. But how sweet it is to be with Him!"

Someone had given Lucy a picture of the Sacred Heart of Jesus. She gave it to Jacinta, who kept it constantly, and often kissed it.

"I am kissing the Heart of Him whom I love above all. I wish I also had a picture of the Heart of Mary. I would be so pleased to have the two together."

Nailed to her bed, Jacinta suffered happily. Her resignation and spirit of sacrifice became even more intense, as if, feeling her end draw near, she meant to make a supreme effort to win a beautiful crown.

Lucy's visits were her one great happiness. She could confide to her the apostolic ambition of her heart, her love for Jesus and Mary, her desire to spread it in all hearts.

"It won't be long before I go to heaven! You, Lucy, will remain on earth to spread the news that our Lord wants the whole world to have devotion to the Immaculate Heart of Mary. When you have to speak, don't hide yourself! Tell the whole world that God wants to grant His graces through the mediation of the Immaculate Heart of Mary; that we must not hesitate to ask them through her; that the Heart of Jesus wants to be venerated along with the Immaculate Heart of Mary; that men must ask that Immaculate Heart

for peace, because God has confided it to her. If I could only put
into all hearts what I feel here within me, what makes me love
the Hearts of Jesus and Mary so! . . . "

When other children from the hamlet came to see her, she tried
to inspire them with that love. She let boys and girls come into her
room, only, though, if they were younger than herself.

She taught them prayers and hymns. Then she would play with
them, sitting on her bed, or else on the floor in the middle of the
room, if she were up when they came. Then she would make
them say their beads and advise them never again to offend our
Lord so as not to go to hell.

Some children would spend a whole morning or a whole afternoon with her. "When they had gone," said Lucy, "they didn't dare
come back, as if respect kept them away. They would come for
me and ask me to introduce them. Others waited in front of the
door till my aunt or Jacinta would call them and ask them to
come in."

The women of the village would come to see her, too. They
would sit by her bed and sew or knit, while their little children
played with the invalid. If a word against charity or any other
virtue escaped them, Jacinta would gently reprove them.

Out of curiosity or devotion, some people came a long way to
see her. They admired her unalterable patience for, though her
sufferings were evidently great, she never complained or demanded
anything. Before these strangers she was usually very serious and
silent. Some would stay a long time near her bed, happy just to
be at her side. No matter how minute their questions were, she
would answer briefly and simply, without showing impatience or
displeasure. But when Lucy came, she could speak her mind: "My
head aches from hearing those people. Now I can't run away or
hide myself, so I have more sacrifices to offer our Lord."

All those visitors, standing at her side, experienced something
supernatural. A priest once said to Lucy, after a visit of this kind
while Francis was still living: "What impressed me most is the
innocence, the sincerity, of Francis and Jacinta."

A fellow priest who accompanied him said: "I don't know what

I feel near those little children. It seems to me to be something supernatural. It does my soul good to speak with them."

TO SUFFER MORE

But little Jacinta's sickness was steadily growing worse. Soon the doctor spoke of complications of pleurisy that would require treatment in a hospital. Jacinta was expecting this. She even thought the moment had come for the separation from her mother and from Lucy. Her heavenly Friend had told her she would remain alone in a hospital to which her mother would send her.

"If you could only come with me, Lucy! I'm going over there to suffer all alone!"

She was admitted to the Hospital of St. Augustin at Ourém, on condition that her parents paid a slight board, and she remained there through July and August of 1919.

Whenever her mother came to see her, she asked her to bring Lucy, as a special favor. And while Olimpia left her for errands in town, the two children told each other the anxieties of their souls.

"She was happy," says Sister Lucy, "to suffer for the love of God and for the Immaculate Heart of Mary, for sinners and for the Holy Father. She could not speak of anything else."

After two months in the hospital, Jacinta came home just as sick as she was before. A fistula had opened on the left side which caused her intense suffering. The daily dressing was very painful, but she never complained.

Not to be able to escape from curious people who came to question her was a fresh cause of pain. "How much rather would I like to go and say the rosary on the mountain!"

The wound was growing worse every day. Soon the pus came so abundantly that by bending she could make it flow into a little bowl. Never a complaint, however; always the same sweet smile.

She not only suffered what came; she made herself suffer even more! When asked if she needed anything, she would answer: "Thank you, I need nothing."

And when the others had scarcely left the room, she would

whisper to Lucy: "I'm very thirsty! but I want to offer it to Jesus for sinners."

She did not like milk at all, but she took it readily, so that her mother said that now her taste had changed and she liked milk. On certain nights she offered the sacrifice of not changing her position in bed.

Just as when her health was good, she continued to get up to recite the angel's prayer. But she had grown so weak that she could not bend her head to the floor without falling. So she was satisfied simply to kneel.

When Lucy told this to Father Jacinto Ferreira, pastor of Olival, he sent word to her cousin to remain in bed to pray. And she obeyed, because Lucy told her "Jesus loves people who follow the advice of the Father Pastor."

Sometimes her mother, on coming in, would find her very still and thoughtful, with her face buried in her hands. "What were you thinking about so long, my little girl?"

She would answer only with a smile, and soon fall back into the same recollection. But she would entrust her thoughts to Lucy: "I was thinking of our Lord, of the Blessed Virgin, of sinners, and of . . . [something probably relating to the secret]. I love to think!"

Does not the Holy Ghost say that He holds delightful colloquies with the innocent and the simple of heart?

AT LISBON

During one of these meditations the Blessed Virgin appeared again. Jacinta was not surprised at these visits from her heavenly Mother. This time she came to announce her final Calvary and to prepare her for it.

"She told me," Jacinta said to Lucy, "that I shall go to Lisbon, to another hospital. I will not see you, nor my parents, nor my relatives again. After many sufferings, I shall die alone. She told me, too, not to be afraid, because she will come and take me to heaven."

With tears flowing down her cheeks, Jacinta kissed her cousin.

"I shall never see you again. You will not come to see me. Listen: pray for me very much, for I shall die alone." This thought of "dying alone" never left her now.

One day Lucy found her hugging an image of the Blessed Virgin and saying: "Oh, my good Mother in heaven, must I really die quite lonely?"

"Why should you care, since the Blessed Virgin is coming to take you?"

"That's true! I don't know why, but there are times when I forget that she will come to get me."

And Lucy sometimes heard her say: "O Jesus, I think you can convert many sinners, this sacrifice is so great!"

An unforeseen circumstance came to hasten the accomplishment of our Lady's predictions. About mid-January, a well-known Lisbon doctor, a specialist in ophthalmology, came on pilgrimage to the Cova da Iria. He wished to see the children. Finding little Jacinta in a pitiful condition, he insisted on her being brought to Lisbon, assuring everyone that an operation might save her.

The parents objected that the little patient had only one wish: to join her little brother as soon as possible, "at home with the Blessed Virgin," and that the best care would be as useless as in the hospital at Ourém, since the Blessed Virgin was to come to get her.

The doctor replied that the best way to know whether the Blessed Virgin wanted her was to take the best possible care of her. "After that we shall see what the Blessed Virgin will do." And he offered to pay all the expenses.

Since Olimpia constantly refused to let her darling child go, the doctor spoke to the Baron of Alvayàzere, who spoke to the new pastor of Fàtima. Olimpia was called to the priest's house and finally consented. Jacinta heard the discussions but made no objection, because she knew her destiny was to go to Lisbon, to die there.

"The parting," writes Sister Lucy, "was heartbreaking." The child kissed her over and over, with tears streaming from her eyes, and saying: "Pray for me constantly, till I get to heaven. When

I am there, I shall pray for you without stopping. Never tell the secret to anyone, even though they want to kill you. Love Jesus and the Immaculate Heart of Mary and make many sacrifices for sinners."

A rich family of Lisbon had been asked to receive the little patient and to keep her until she was admitted to the hospital. But on seeing the real state of the child, they refused to take her into their home.

So Olimpia went to an orphanage, near the Church of Our Lady of Miracles, which was conducted by a secularized Franciscan religious, Sister Maria Purification Godinho. This nun had read about Fàtima and had asked God for the grace to know the children. Now she was being asked to receive one of these very children among her boarders. Of course she received Jacinta with great joy and a most generous charity.

Jacinta had scarcely entered when a lady came to see her, asked for a prayer, and left her about twenty-five dollars, which she handed over at once to the nun. Her board was thus paid for beforehand.

Sister Godinho had about twenty boarders then, nearly all of whom were "free"; so they called their benefactress "godmother." Jacinta gave her the same name and called the orphanage "Our Lady of Fàtima's House."

The patient was there for barely fifteen days. She left an imperishable remembrance of her sweetness, piety, patience, and modesty, her spirit of prayer, and especially her touching gratitude. Her little companions were much impressed by her example.

It made her very happy to live under the same roof with her beloved Jesus. She spoke often of Him, expressing a great desire for Holy Communion, and, according to Sister Godinho's declaration, received it every day. She would often go to the chapel and remain there a long time with her eyes fixed on the tabernacle.

The Blessed Virgin appeared to her several times; some accounts mention apparitions of St. Joseph and her guardian angel as well.

One day when she was in bed and the directress had come to see her, she said: "Come later, godmother. Now I am waiting for the Blessed Virgin." And she looked fixedly, as if transfigured, in the direction from which the heavenly visitor was coming.

Neither imagination nor fever had anything to do with these visions. The child's thoughts after these colloquies are a sufficient proof of it. They are of things far above her age and her rudimentary instruction.

Her godmother, who collected some of these thoughts, asked her one day who had taught her these things.

"The Blessed Virgin," she answered. "Some I found myself though. I so love to think!"

Another proof that the revelations mentioned by Jacinta were true is that many prophecies made to the child before her death were fulfilled afterward.

She told her godmother about the approaching death of two of her sisters, whom her mother, Olimpia, would not allow to become nuns. She said that the nun's desire to go to Fàtima would be realized, but only after her (Jacinta's) death. Sister Godinho did accompany the child's remains to Ourém.

To a physician who asked her to pray for him from heaven, Jacinta said: "You will follow me very soon!"

Another physician drew near and asked her to pray for him and for one of his daughters. Jacinta promised; then, after a long look, she said: "You will both follow me; your daughter first, then you."

The two predictions were verified. Other examples are quoted, among which are singular cases of penetration of conscience.

THE OPERATION AND DEATH

Jacinta always said that an operation for her would be useless, for our Lady had said she would soon come to get her. She would have loved to die in "Our Lady of Fàtima's House," and the godmother, too, would have wished it. But Dr. Lisboa was inflexible. He asked his friend, Dr. Leonardo de Castro Freire, director of the Dona Stefania hospital, to operate.

On the Feast of the Purification, after confession and Communion, she left for the hospital. Her last farewell, with more

tears than words, was to "hidden Jesus" in the tabernacle of the
little church.

At Dona Stefania, doctors and nurses scolded Sister Godinho
for having kept such a sick child among her pupils. Jacinta defended her godmother.

She was admitted to the children's section, and it was known
that she was one of the seers of Fàtima. But the staff has no recollection of this patient; she was just a number, like the others.

Fortunately, Sister Godinho and a benefactress came to see her
every day. She received a visit from the orphanage physician, Dr.
Cardoso Tavares; and her mother and father came to Lisbon once
to see her.

Jacinta kept repeating that the operation would be useless. She
got someone to write to Lucy: "The Blessed Virgin came to see
me again. She told me the day and the hour when she would
come for me, and told me to be very good (bien sage)."

The hospital surroundings were very different from those at
the orphanage. The prediction of holy Mary and the little girl's own
somber presentiments were to be realized all right. She was alone,
and she would die alone.

The operation was performed on the tenth of February by the
chief surgeon, Dr. Castro Freire, assisted by Dr. Elvas. Because of
her extreme weakness, they dared not administer chloroform, only
a local anesthetic. She cried bitterly when they took off her clothes.

They cut away two ribs on the left side, which left a wound as
large as the hand.

When the wound was dressed she had spasmodic pains, but she
never once lost her angelic patience: "O my good Mother! O my
good Mother!" she would moan when the pain was most intense.

She would encourage herself frequently by repeating: "Patience!
We must all suffer to gain heaven!"

And in the bottom of her heart, she would doubtless repeat: "O
Jesus, all for Thy love and for the conversion of sinners! You can
convert many, for this sacrifice costs so much!"

Four days before her death (Monday, February 16), she spoke
to her godmother of her particularly agonizing pain.

The next day, however, while she was exhorting her to patience, Jacinta replied: "Listen, godmother; now I don't complain any more. Our Lady appeared to me again. She will soon come for me! She has taken away all my pain!" From that hour she never complained and no sign of suffering appeared on her face.

She added that the Blessed Virgin had looked very sad this time, and had even told her the cause of her sorrow: "The sins which lead the greatest number of souls to perdition are the sins of the flesh. It is necessary to give up luxury, not to remain obstinately in sin, as they have done until now. Great penance is indispensable." And Jacinta added: "Oh! I feel so sad for our Lady! I feel so sad!"

On Friday, the twentieth of February, at about six o'clock in the evening, she said that she was going to die, and asked for the last sacraments. About eight o'clock, the pastor of Holy Angels Church, Father Fereira dos Reis, came to hear her confession and spoke of returning the next morning for Holy Viaticum. Jacinta insisted that he should not delay it. She was going to die. The priest believed all the same that he could wait until morning. But that very evening, about 10:30, with only the night nurse in attendance, she breathed her last in perfect peace.

A WHITE MONUMENT

Her godmother dressed that innocent little body, which had suffered so much for the conversion of sinners, in a white First Communion dress with a blue sash, as the child had requested.

At the news of her death, there was a subscription among the Catholics of Fàtima living in Lisbon to have her remains brought back to her native country.

After the funeral service at the Church of the Holy Angels, which drew a large crowd, the coffin was brought to the sacristy to await the transfer. So many people came to see the body of the little seer and to touch-beads and medals to it, that the coffin had to be left open. It remained there four days.

"Lying in her little coffin," says one of the guards, "she seemed to be alive, with pink cheeks and lips. She was most beautiful.

When the people came up to that coffin they were carried away by enthusiasm, admiration, almost delirium. It exhaled a sweet odor, like that of exquisite flowers; the most incredulous could not doubt it."

Dr. Enrico Lisboa finds the fact even more surprising, considering the infectious nature of the sickness, and that the coffin was left open for several days.

On the twenty-fourth of February, about noon, the body was placed in a leaden coffin, with quicklime, according to the rule. A numerous retinue accompanied it to the station. It was taken by train to Chão de Maçâs and buried, not at Fàtima, but at Ourém in the family vault of the Baron of Alvayàzere.

Fifteen years later, on September 12, 1935, despite the opposition of the family of Alvayàzere, who attributed many graces received by them to the presence of Mary's little confidant, the bishop of Leiria had Jacinta's remains brought to the Fàtima cemetery. There, a little white vault had been built where the body of Francis already rested.

The procession which brought the precious remains stopped at the Cova da Iria, where the faithful had already arrived for the next day's pilgrimage. The archbishop of Evora celebrated the Requiem Mass. Then a fervent retinue accompanied the coffin to the cemetery.

And now, before the white vault containing the bodies of Mary's two little friends, the prelates and princes of the Church do not hesitate to kneel and beg protection for themselves, for their dioceses, and for the groups of Catholic Action.

SOME OF JACINTA'S LAST WORDS[*]

"Dear godmother, avoid luxury; never seek riches; rather, love holy poverty and silence.

"Be full of charity, even toward the wicked. Say no evil of anyone and avoid backbiters.

"Be very patient: patience leads to paradise.

---

[*] Sister Godinho's Notes.

"Mortification and sacrifice please Jesus very much.

"I would willingly enter a convent; but I am better pleased to go to heaven as soon as possible. To be a nun, one must be very pure in soul and body."

"And do you know what it is to be pure?" asked her godmother.

"I know. I know. To be pure in body means to be chaste. To be pure in soul means to commit no sin, not to look at what one should not see, not to steal, not to lie, to always tell the truth, even when it costs."

"But who taught you all those things?"

"The Blessed Virgin. Some, I found by myself. I so love to think."

On Sin

"The sins that throw most souls into hell are sins of impurity.

"There are certain fashions that offend our Lord very much.

"Persons who serve our Lord should not follow the fashions. The Church has no fashions. Our Lord is always the same.

"Many sins, and very grave sins, are committed in the world.

"If men knew what eternity is, they would try to change their life."

On Priests

"My dear godmother, pray very much for sinners! Pray very much for priests! Pray very much for religious!

"Priests must be pure, very pure. Priests should busy themselves only with the things of the Church and souls."

On the War

"The Blessed Virgin said there are many wars and discords in the world; wars are only punishments for the sins of the world.

"The Blessed Virgin can no longer restrain her Son's arm over the world.

"Penance is necessary! If men repented, our Lord would still forgive them, but if they don't change their life, the chastisement will follow."

It seems that, in saying these things, the Blessed Virgin showed herself sad, for the child repeated: "Poor Holy Mother, she makes me feel so sad, so sad!"

Sister Godinho writes, in connection with this thought: "There is question here of a great chastisement, of which she often spoke to me in secret. May our Lord have pity on us!

"In a few years we shall see many things in the world. It is true that our Lord has said: 'If men will repent . . . all things are in our hands.' My God, have pity on us!"

On Public Authorities

"My dear godmother, pray very much for the governments. If the government would leave the Church in peace and give liberty to holy religion, it would be blessed by God."

19

LUCY'S VOCATION

THE BISHOP AND THE SEER

"It is good to hide the secret of a king" (Tob. 12:7). This word of the Scripture seems to apply to certain elements of the mystery of Fàtima that Providence has not yet explained. It applies in particular to the life of the only survivor of the three seers, Sister Mary of the Dolors, and it is perhaps premature to speak of it to the general reader.

She herself wishes to be hidden and forgotten. Unless providential circumstances oblige her to speak again, the whole story of the revelations may not be told until her death.

This chapter can satisfy the curiosity of the reader only as far as it concerns the exterior and apparent life of Lucy of Aljustrel. But from this point of view alone, it is of sufficient interest.

After the death of her two cousins, Lucy continued to come alone to the place of the apparitions. Simple and modest, she would say the rosary with the crowd of pilgrims. Because of the total absence of clergy, this girl of thirteen seemed to be, to a certain extent, the religious guide of the multitudes flocking to the Cova da Iria.

Her own vocation of victim had not ended. The death of Francis, followed three months later by that of her own father, and shortly after by that of Jacinta and two other cousins, had crushed her heart. She suffered from what she called her "solitude," that is, her separation from her two closest friends. She suffered also from the fervent crowds, so naturally indiscreet; from the silence of the

religious authority; from the sometimes violent hostility of certain
fanatics or freethinkers. She was even struck in the street, because
the rector had announced publicly that he intended to leave the
parish where he received so many annoyances.

She suffered, too, from feeling left alone to accomplish the mission confided to her by our Lady, to make her divine Son known
and loved. And how bitter were the thoughts aroused in her by
certain comments on the death of her father and of her cousins!

"It was necessary to make those little ones disappear," said
some. "In the end they would have told who got up this comedy."

"They'll all have to disappear, the children and the parents,"
said others. "As long as some remain alive, the thing can't be
crushed."

Then, suddenly, about the middle of June, 1921, Lucy herself
suddenly disappeared. It was a kind of scandal in the country.
Endless contradictory reports came from friends as well as enemies.
The freethinking mayor of Ourém thought it his duty to intervene.
He sent for Antonio's widow to do some explaining.

Maria Rosa answered with her usual directness: "My daughter is
where she wanted to go and where I want her to be. I have no
other explanation to give you."

The mayor did not insist.

Lucy had, in fact, been entered in an unassuming boarding school
at Vilar (near Porto), managed by the Sisters of St. Dorothy. This
was the result of a decision reached mutually by the bishop of
Leiria, the new pastor of Fàtima, Lucy's family, and the seer
herself.

As soon as the bishop, Msgr. José da Silva, had become acquainted with his new diocese, he realized he could not leave to a
girl of thirteen the responsibility for the religious movement at
the Cova da Iria. Nor could he leave this child exposed to the
curiosity or even malignity of the crowds, or — who could tell? —
even to temptations of pride.

She should also receive instruction since, as she said, the vision
had suggested it.

Then, by withdrawing her for a time, during her studies, both her feelings and those of the pilgrims might be better tested. It would stop the many objections of the adversaries of Fàtima and of religion.

Called before the bishop, Lucy answered all questions simply, frankly, and in perfect conformity to Catholic faith. Moreover, she was really anxious to leave her native place, to get away from the crowd, to live closer to our Blessed Lady and to the two little friends who preceded her to paradise.

Two days before her departure, the good and kind bishop made his final recommendations: "My child, you must keep a perfect secret concerning your destination."

"Yes, my Lord."

"You will be given a new name. That will be the only one you will use."

"Yes, my Lord."

"You will keep the Fàtima apparitions to yourself."

"Yes, my Lord."

Her fidelity to those promises, given with the calm assurance of a soul sure of itself, were to be the conclusive assurance for the bishop that the shepherdess of Aljustrel was worthy of her role of confidante of heaven's Queen.

FIFTEEN YEARS OF SILENCE

Lucy was to keep this silence till the bishop himself revealed her identity. Even now, her most intense desire would be to fall back into that silence and shadow in which she succeeded in wrapping herself for so long.

On the eve of her departure, she had gone secretly to each of those dear places to say good-by forever, especially to the Fàtima cemetery and the Cova da Iria.

At the *Asilo de Vilar* (this was Lucy's new home), the seer was grudgingly received by a directress who disbelieved in the Fàtima apparitions, and who regarded her at first as a "savage from the woods," accepting her only at the bishop's request. She could be trusted to keep the secret of Lucy's identity; but for fear that the girl herself might violate it, she imposed her own orders upon her:

"When they ask your name, you will say: Maria-das-Dores (Mary of the Dolors)."

"Yes, Madam."

"About what happened or is happening at Fàtima you will never say a word, neither by way of question nor of answer."

"No, Madam."

Lucy kept her promise so well that she never uttered a word about her visions or the pilgrimages, not even to her mother when Maria Rosa came to see her, once at Porto and once at Braga.

Mary of the Dolors remained four years at Vilar. At first, in the company of her classmates, she displayed her character as that of a real little mountaineer. But she soon deserved to be received as a Child of Mary and to be trusted with the little ones' dormitory.

She succeeded fairly well with her studies and, had it not been necessary to hide her name, she could have passed the government examinations successfully. Besides her class subjects, she learned domestic economy, embroidery, and typewriting.

During those four years, no companion, or teacher, or visitor, not a single person, said anything to Lucy about the things happening at Fàtima. If, by chance, anyone asked the portress if Lucy of Fàtima was to be found in that convent, the answer came with perfectly good faith: "We have no Lucy here."

The seer therefore knew nothing, unless told by revelation, about the wonderful development of the oratory of the Cova da Iria, and of the miraculous spreading of devotion to Mary that was transforming the whole country. She did not know either of the marvelous flow of water, at the very place where, on May 13, 1917, she was transfixed to the spot by the second flash of lightning. She knew nothing of the miracles of which everybody spoke. For the directress kept close watch on all news of that kind, and she herself kept still.

She sought to be unnoticed, unperceived, among the pupils. She was always calm and even tempered — but she could play and joke. Of course, she would not forget the "poor sinners" any more than formerly, but now no one noticed it. A few of her teachers and companions did recognize her particular devotion to our Lady.

One day, she said to the directress: "I would like to be a Sister of St. Dorothy."

"You are very young, my child! And why would you like to be a Sister?"

"To be freer to go to the chapel."

"But you are too young. You will have to wait."

Lucy was silent and waited more than a year. When she was eighteen the superior said: "You don't think at all now of being a religious?"

"I always think of it! I wish for it! I want to be a nun!"

"Then?"

"You told me to wait. So I waited."

To make her novitiate, Mary of the Dolors now went to Tuy, in Spanish Galicia, where the provincial house of the Dorothy Sisters had gone into exile after the revolution of 1910.

This order was founded in 1834 by the Blessed Paula Frassinetti (1809–1882), who was beatified in 1930.

Lucy was immediately admitted as a postulant, without passing through the preliminary step of aspirant. This she had begged of God in the summer of 1925.

During the next three years she studied the religious life and the rules of her congregation. The sisters are classed in two categories: teachers and coadjutrices. She could aspire no lower — she chose to be a coadjutrix. On October 2, 1926, she received the black robe of the Dorothy Sisters with the white veil of the novices.

Here, too, her only ambition was to appear in all things "like the others." She succeeded perfectly, so perfectly that only the Reverend Mother knew that Sister Mary of the Dolors was the seer of Fàtima. In Portugal it was vaguely known that Lucy of Jesus was in Spain, in some convent of Galicia or Asturias.

Toward the end of her novitiate, in a corridor of the mother house she came across a picture of Our Lady of Fàtima. "Well!" she murmured, blushing and putting down her eyes, "just as I thought!"

Another time, she found a medal that was forgotten on a bench. It was Our Lady of Fàtima, with the three little shepherds! This time she cried with all her heart: "My God! Why did you choose me? Through mercy! But why not anyone but me?"

When Lucy was twenty-one, she pronounced her first vows, October 30, 1928. Rumors were spreading, however, that the seer of Fàtima was a Sister of St. Dorothy at Tuy. The religious there were often questioned by people who wanted to find out where she was. Knowing nothing at all themselves, they could give no information. Lucy herself was questioned, but she had sufficient wit to neither tell her secret nor violate the truth.

WHOLLY TO GOD

In her new surroundings, Lucy continued to edify her companions by her perfect obedience, her deep humility, her spirit of prayer, and that unfailing energy at work which made up the main trait in her character.

After six years, on October 3, 1934, she pronounced her final vows. For the first time, after fourteen years, she found herself surrounded with love. Her mother, two of her sisters, some cousins, and a friend came from faraway Fàtima to celebrate that great day.

More than that, Msgr. Correia da Silva wished to come himself to preside at the ceremony. By this action he finally was breaking down the wall of silence and shadow which had surrounded the seer. Besides, who could doubt now that her humility would bear the strain.

Maria Rosa insisted three times that her dear Lucy — she no longer accused her of deceiving people — should tell her what present she would like best. Sister Mary of the Dolors asked for flowers and . . . bees! So, her mother brought her a great bunch of home flowers and a hive filled with golden bees.

A few days later, the newly professed sister was sent to Pontevedra, to a young girls' boarding school called Our Lady of Dolors College. Here she found again the directress who had received her coldly at the Asilo de Vilar. She still avoided speaking to her of

Fàtima and wished to treat her in all things like the other coad-jutrices, but she knew now that the Blessed Virgin had a special love for Lucy.

When asked what she thought of that sister, she answered: "She is extraordinary in the ordinary," which signified that the seer of Fàtima, without being in any way different from her companions, fulfilled every duty to perfection and enjoyed a deep interior life.

In her spirituality her preference went to the "little way" of St. Thérèse of Lisieux, and to the "joyful submission" of St. John Berchmans. More, perhaps, than in books or even in the advice of her confessor, she found her principle of direction in the words of the Lady who had told her long before: "I will not abandon you. My Immaculate Heart will be your refuge and your way to God."

Do you suppose that Lucy of Jesus was not interested in all that took place at Fàtima? By prayer and sacrifice, she lived only for that. No one noticed it, however, even though they knew who she was.

On the thirteenth of each month, in the splendid sanctuary built on her father's old pasture, no pilgrim was more fervent than the little Dorothy Sister of Pontevedra. She followed in thought all the phases of those innumerable gatherings. In this way, while applying herself to all her daily tasks, as did the others, she could say she spent her days at Fàtima, though, with her own eyes, she had seen neither the sanctuary nor the pilgrimage. Her whole life belonged to Our Lady of Fàtima. Could she for a moment forget the words of the Lady of Light, or the promise she made to suffer and pray for the conversion of sinners, or the secret she was to keep sealed in her heart while living among men?

Happy Francis and Jacinta, who had been able to reveal it to the other saints! One could say Lucy lived in the intimacy of those invisible companions. So, what a joy for her to obey Msgr. Correia da Silva when he asked her to reveal the virtues of her little cousin, Jacinta!

"There was question," she declared in her letter to the bishop, "of the most intimate friend of my childhood, to whose company

I partly owe the preservation of my innocence." She added, "I hope that the Lord will grant her, for the glory of the Most Blessed Virgin, the halo of sanctity. Jacinta was only a child, but she already knew how to practice virtue and prove her love for God and the Blessed Virgin by sacrifice. It was wonderful to see how perfectly she had understood the spirit of prayer and sacrifice recommended by our Lady herself. Because of that and many other things, I really think she was a saint."

Before the twenty-fifth anniversary of the apparitions the bishop of Leiria thought the moment had come to reveal some details the general public still ignored. He asked the seer to write down all she could remember about Francis and Jacinta, and an exact narration of the apparitions, "without omitting anything that can actually be manifested."

In response to this request came two new documents, amounting to about sixty typewritten pages.

This new act of obedience was a hard sacrifice for the humble religious. She wrote: "I think I have written all that your Excellency asked of me. Up to this point I had done all I could to hide whatever was most intimate in the apparitions of Our Lady at the Cova da Iria. Every time I had been obliged to speak I had lightly glided over these affairs, fearing to reveal what I so profoundly desired to keep hidden. But, since obedience obliges me to speak — well, here are the facts. And now, I remain, like a skeleton in a museum, stripped of my own life, to recall to visitors the misery and nothingness of all that passes.

"May our good Lord and the Immaculate Heart of Mary accept the sacrifices they have deigned to ask of me, to renew in souls the spirit of faith, of confidence, and of love."

From these last writings of Lucy are drawn especially the apparitions of the angels to the little shepherds, important details about the first three apparitions, some characteristic traits concerning Francis, and certain prophetic visions granted to Jacinta.

Lucy has but one ambition now: to love our Lord and His holy Mother a little better every day, so that she might prove herself less unworthy of that heaven once promised her by Mary.

In the meantime, many assure us that her heavenly Friend has granted her new revelations. Some day, perhaps, they will become known for the greater glory of God and of His most holy Mother, Our Lady of Fàtima.

20

ATMOSPHERIC PRODIGIES

"SIGNS IN THE HEAVENS"

One characteristic of the apparitions at Fàtima is that the onlookers were aware of an invisible presence by certain exterior manifest signs. The number, variety, and strangeness of these signs astonished certain people, especially those who had not witnessed them.

But our Lord Himself made use of miracles to prove His teaching. The Gospels, especially that of St. John, bear witness to this in every page. Jesus of Nazareth, says St. Peter, was "a man approved of God among you by miracles and wonders and signs, which God did through him in the midst of you, as you know" (Acts 2:22). Our Lord granted these exterior, sensational marks of His divinity to sincere souls, through the multiplication of loaves, the calming of the tempest, His walking on the waters, His transfiguration, His raising of the dead, His own resurrection, etc. At the end of the world, our Lord Himself tells us, "there shall be signs in the sun, and in the moon, and in the stars" (Luke 21:25).

Our Lady was most generous with "signs" at Fàtima. One can only conclude from it how anxious she was to draw attention to the message she was giving the whole world by means of the three little shepherds. The strength of miracles contrasts with the weakness of Mary's confidants. She chose innocent and defenseless witnesses. She must therefore authenticate their testimony by incontestable proofs.

DURING THE FIRST FOUR APPARITIONS

On May 13, 1917, the children were alone. They spoke of a *first flash* of lightning while they were "building" their little house on the top of the hill, then of a *second flash* while they were running down the slope, and finally of a *halo* that enveloped them, the tree, and the vision of our Lady herself.

Here, the flash merely gives notice of the vision. It would seem to have been the same in the subsequent apparitions.

Usually, these flashes were perceived by the seers alone; but at other times, as on the thirteenth of August, the whole multitude saw them.

On the thirteenth of August, the fourth apparition should have taken place, but the children had been kidnaped and could not be present. Yet the Blessed Virgin willed that the angry crowd should be pacified. This time, they all witnessed the two flashes of lightning accompanied by two distinct claps of thunder.

Then the usual light cloud was formed about the holm tree, and remained for the entire length of time taken by the previous apparitions, as if the Blessed Virgin had really been there.

When our Lady appeared at Valinhos, on the nineteenth of August, it was the yellow tint of the atmosphere and not the flash which warned Lucy and Francis of the approaching vision. But Lucy saw the two flashes afterward. John, Francis' brother, also saw the peculiar change in the sunlight. He went to fetch his little sister, and on his return noticed the same phenomenon that lasted until the end of the scene, of which he was the only witness aside from the actors themselves. Then he heard a great detonation like the sound of a bomb.

That same day, our Lady rewarded her little friends for their constancy in prison by a charming surprise. John had cut down the branch on which the Lady had seemed to rest. And as they passed her uncle Antonio's house, Jacinta gave it to her aunt, Maria Rosa, who was standing on her threshold. While she held it, all the assistants noticed a fragrant, unknown perfume that pervaded the house and the whole neighborhood. This so influenced Lucy's parents that they began to believe seriously in their daughter's sincerity.

THE LUMINOUS GLOBE AT THE FIFTH APPARITION

On the thirteenth of September, the Lady came back for the fifth time. This visit was the occasion for still more surprising marvels, as though the Queen of Heaven, happy to see this crowd coming at the word of the children, wished to reward or encourage their good will.

According to all the witnesses, and there were about thirty thousand, the radiance of the sun diminished till the stars could be seen, and it assumed a golden tint as on the previous occasions. But immediately after this double phenomenon an altogether new wonder was manifested.

Here is the account of a priest, Rev. João (John) Quaresma, who was later to become vicar general of Leiria. He had come there incognito with his friend, Rev. Manuel do Carmo Gois. They were following the events from the top of a hill, somewhat apart from the crowd. Later they regretted that they had not drawn nearer to the tree of the apparitions.

"The people," writes Father Quaresma, "were still praying. Suddenly, we heard exclamations of surprise and joy. Thousands of arms were raised, pointing to the same part of the heavens.

" 'Look! There! She is there! She is coming — there! Do you see?'

" 'Oh! yes! I see! How beautiful! How beautiful!'

"There was not a cloud in the blue heavens. I looked in the direction indicated, and my friend said to me, teasing: 'Well! You too are looking into the air!'

"Then, to my great surprise, I saw clearly and distinctly, a globe of light moving from east to west, slipping slowly, majestically, through space.

"With my hand I made a sign to my friend who was making fun of me. He raised his eyes and was happy to see this unexpected apparition for himself.

"Then, suddenly, the globe with its wonderful light vanished. My friend also could see it no longer. Near us, however, a young girl dressed like Lucy and about her age continued to cry out joyfully: 'I see it! I can still see it! Now it is going down to the foot of the hill' — that is toward the holm tree, where Mary showed herself."

Then the events of the fifth apparition took place. While the children were talking to the invisible being, the people could perceive the white mist surrounding the holm tree and the seers, and the shower of white flowers falling from heaven.

"A short time after, exactly the usual time of the apparition," writes the vicar general, "the same little girl cried out again, pointing with her finger: 'There! There! Now she is going up again!' And the child continued to see and point with her hand to the globe of light, till it had disappeared in the direction of the sun, sinking into its light.

"From the enthusiasm of the people, we could suppose that all but a few individuals had seen the same thing, for from all sides rose shouts of joy and acclamations in honor of Mary.

" 'What do you think of that globe?' I then asked my friend.

" 'That it was the Blessed Virgin,' he answered without hesitation.

"That was my conviction, too. The little shepherds had seen the Mother of God; we were allowed merely to see the vehicle — if you may call it that — which had brought her from heaven to the inhospitable Serra de Aire.

"We were truly happy. With transports of joy my colleague went from group to group, in the Cova da Iria or on the road, asking them what they had seen. These people belonged to many different social categories but all affirmed the phenomena we had witnessed with the same certainty. We left, exceedingly satisfied, but determined to return on the thirteenth of October."

But there had been exceptions. Not everyone had seen the globe of brilliant whiteness. The Viscount of Montelo, who was there, says: "Some people observed the phenomenon for a longer time than others. I did not see it at all, I am sorry to say." One woman, a fervent Catholic who stood beside the more favored priests, said sorrowfully: "I saw nothing at all."

Why did Mary deny her favors that day to a few faithful ones while, in the following month, she showered them on everyone present, and even on many who were far away? Mystery of her mercy! In any case, the inequality of vision excludes the hypothesis of collective hallucination, for among the very ones who did not see were some who would have heartily wished to do so.

THE "DANCE" OF THE SUN

The great prodigy which, for the Portuguese, stamps the whole mystery of Fàtima as divine is the "sign of God," that solar phenomenon which followed the sixth and last great apparition.

In his pastoral letter of approbation the bishop of Leiria speaks of it as follows:

"The solar phenomenon of October 13, 1917, was the most marvelous of all and the one that made the greatest impression upon all those who had the happiness of witnessing it.

"The three children had announced beforehand the place and time at which it was to happen, and their prediction had been circulated all through Portugal. Thus, despite the bad, rainy weather, thousands and thousands of people had gathered at Fàtima at the time of the last apparition. And this entire crowd assisted at all the manifestations of the king of the skies who thus rendered homage to the Queen of Heaven and Earth, more brilliant than the sun at the highest point of his splendor, as says the *Canticle of Canticles* (6:9).

"This solar phenomenon, which no astronomical observatory registered and which consequently was not natural, was observed by that multitude of people of every category and social class, by believers and unbelievers, by reporters from all the Portuguese newspapers, and even by people many miles away. This circumstance destroys all explanation by collective illusion."

That is the bare fact, told by a particularly authoritative pen, in an official, even historic, document.

"But how admit," some may protest who hear of it for the first time, "that the sun 'danced'? If it had, it should have been visible over the whole hemisphere. And it would no sooner have begun its movement than the whole planetary system would have been so completely upset that our poor earth would have completely disappeared."

The very fact that the phenomenon was not registered by the observatories, says Msgr. José da Silva, clearly proves that it was due only to the will of her who had promised a visible sign of her presence.

If, at that moment, the spectators could actually have thought that the sun itself was being agitated by these giratory movements or by these zigzag bounds — which made them think of the end of the world — then on reflection, as soon as the phenomenon had ceased, everyone must have realized that nothing had changed in the relations of our planet with the sun.

To be favored by a "great miracle," as promised by the Lady and announced by the children in the month of July, it was not necessary that the sun should really dance. It was sufficient that the assistants should really see what would be for them the proof, the "sign" of the truthfulness of the children.

Besides, it was evident that the vision of this sign was not a purely subjective thing. It was not possible that the sensations of this crowd of seventy thousand persons were the fruit only of their imagination. They evidently were purely the result of luminous and atmospheric phenomena exterior to their brains and their eyes. The Queen of Heaven played, so to say, with the rays of the sun to produce these magnificent fireworks.

On the other hand, there is nothing to prevent the conception that God made the sun really "dance" without troubling the solar system. This He could do by modifying the laws of the propagation of light for all the rest of the universe.

In any case, it was an exceptional intervention of divine omnipotence. Whatever means He employed, it was God who manifested His power, in an extraordinary way, at the day and the hour fixed by our Lady's promise.

The objectivity of God's sign is proved, too, by many other considerations.

No one can speak of autosuggestion or collective hallucination, since no one expected or could have expected it. Certainly, the Lady had announced a miracle that everyone would see, but there was nothing to define the nature of it. No one imagined or could have imagined it would consist in making the sun move in this strange way.

One thing only had been announced: the day and the hour of the miracle. And this prediction was accomplished: another proof that the prodigy was the will of her who had announced it.

But there are many other circumstances to be noticed. All morning the sun had been invisible — a rare thing in that country and at that season. How, then, could anyone guess that the sign would come from there?

Those dark clouds that suddenly disappeared! Those clothes, wet all morning, that were suddenly quite dry! Can all that be attributed to the popular imagination?

There were learned men among the witnesses, journalists, free-thinkers, ecclesiastics strongly prejudiced against belief in the apparitions. Even the severe Maria Rosa did not dare call her daughter a liar after that. Were all these people simply played upon?

Leopoldo Nunès says in his book, *Fàtima:* "At the time of the great miracle, there were present some of the most famous writers, artists, scientists, nearly all of them freethinkers, who had come there simply out of curiosity. Now, all those people spoke of the prodigy in the same way as the people from the villages close by."

Another strange thing. It was stated officially that the great prodigy was seen at a distance of two or three miles from the Cova da Iria, and by people who knew nothing of the feelings of the crowd of pilgrims. Other witnesses attest that the solar phenomenon was noticed six, twelve, and even thirty miles away, by those who were not thinking at all of Fàtima.

Here is a letter from Father Ignace Pereira, now a missionary in India:

"Fourteen years have passed, but I retain a vivid recollection of the impression produced on my young mind by the wonderful spectacle of the sun, on the thirteenth of October, 1917.

"I was scarcely nine years old. I was going to school in my native country, in a little village perched on the top of a hill, just opposite the mountain of Fàtima, six or seven miles away. It was about noon when we were alarmed by shouts and exclamations from men and women passing on the public road in front of the school. Our teacher, a good, pious woman but rather nervous, jumped up like a spring and rushed out of the house. All the school children followed after her.

"Outside, the people were gathered in the square, crying, shouting, pointing to the sun, without even hearing the questions poured upon them by our terrified teacher. . . .

"I stared fixedly at the sun. It seemed pale, without its usual flashing light. It looked like a ball of snow turning upon itself. Then, all of a sudden it seemed to come down in zigzags, threatening to fall upon the earth. Scared out of my wits, I rushed into the crowd. Everyone was crying, expecting the end of the world. Close to us was a freethinker, a man who had spent all morning laughing at those leaving for Fàtima. Now he stood there as if paralyzed, stupid, his eyes fixed on the sun. I saw him afterward trembling from head to foot. . . . Finally, raising his eyes to heaven, he fell on his knees in the mud of the road, repeating over and over: 'Holy Virgin! Holy Virgin!' He could say nothing more.

"The people, however, continued to cry and to weep over their sins. Then, from all sides, they crowded into the two village chapels, filling them to overflowing.

"During the long minutes of the solar phenomenon, everything about us reflected all the colors of the rainbow. Our faces were sometimes red, sometimes yellow, sometimes blue, etc., which increased our terror.

"At the end of ten minutes, the sun went back to its place, in the same way in which it had come down, pale and lackluster. When the crowd was sure that all danger had vanished, everybody's face became radiant with joy. They all broke into shouts of thanksgiving, crying: 'A miracle! Praise be to God!' "

This thing was thus judged by every man of good faith: the great miracle of Fàtima was undeniable and the people of Portugal were right in recognizing it as Mary's signature to the story of the six apparitions told by the little shepherds of Aljustrel.

The Lady had promised them a miracle that would make *everyone believe them*. The miracle had occurred, greater than anyone suspected, on the day and at the hour predicted.

All these phenomena mark the apparitions of Fàtima most indelibly. Neither at Lourdes, nor at Pontmain, nor anywhere else, did Mary so unmistakably show her power. Thereby she wished to accredit the account of her seers unmistakably, and fix our inconstant minds upon the whole mystery which her mercy had accomplished at Fàtima.

21

MIRACULOUS CURES

"HEALTH OF THE SICK"

During the prewar period, from May, 1926, to December, 1937, no fewer than 14,735 cases of sickness were registered at the *Bureau of Authentication*. Anyone can appeal to the statistics preserved there.

Even during the course of the apparitions, Lucy and her companions had been requested to submit petitions to our Lady for the cure of certain sick persons. Mary promised repeatedly to cure "some of them." Emphasis, on the other hand, was clearly placed on the fact that for definite reasons it was not in God's providence that *all* should be cured.

The official publication, *La Voz da Fàtima*, had registered more than 800 attested cures already some years ago, among which were tuberculosis, blindness, meningitis, pleurisy, paralysis, ulcers of different kinds considered incurable, bone fractures, cancers, etc.

It will be enough to mention just a very few.

THE MEN

Caries of the Vertebrae (April, 1924)

José de Oliveira, aged twenty-seven, a merchant at Porto, had been suffering for two years from Pott's Disease, with a highly developed abscess in the lumbar region. After many useless treatments, he reached such a state that, to quote from the medical certificate, "when visited by a bone specialist, the latter could not give the family any hope of a delay of more than eight days before the fatal termination of the sickness. Some days later, on the contrary, the patient almost suddenly felt better. The fever disappeared, the fistula ceased to suppurate, the right leg moved without effort, the lumbar pains disappeared, and after a few more days, the sick man asked to leave his bed. Soon he had recovered his former healthy appearance, without the least remnant of weakness or pain."

Thus his physician, Dr. Soares, Junior, testified on January 20, 1925. He did not state, however, that this change took place on the day the patient drank Fàtima water and began to pray with his family to the Blessed Virgin.

A Doctor's Story (*March, 1926*)

The following account is doubly interesting: first for itself, and then because Dr. Acacio da Silva Ribeiro is the subject of it. Understanding that he is a doctor, we can the better appreciate its value. Here is his account slightly summarized from *La Voz da Fàtima:*

"I am absolutely convinced that I was preserved from death only by the intercession of Our Lady of the Rosary of Fàtima, in the accident which occurred to me. . . .

"It all happened on the evening of the ninth of May, 1926, at about half past six, on the road leading to the station of Canas de Senhorim. I was going at great speed on a motorcycle, when suddenly I swerved to avoid a cart. At that moment I heard a violent explosion, and was hurled quite a distance. . . . It was a terrible instant! I heard my last hour ring. As a doctor, I am convinced that my life could have lasted only a few seconds after that terrible fall and the fearful hemorrhages that followed it, unless I were able to stop them at once.

"I thought then of my wife and children, waiting for me some four or five hundred yards away. With that I invoked Our Lady of the Rosary of Fàtima and awaited death, mentally resigning myself to God's will. . . .

"A few moments passed, moments of great anxiety. Seeing that my lucidity of mind still continued, I gained new hope of life and of beholding my family again. There and then I made a promise to Our Lady of Fàtima, and in an outpouring of unspeakable devotion to her I prayed her to help me and preserve my life.

"I must note, too, the following detail. My wife, informed of the accident, had rushed up a few minutes later. But even before coming to my help, she had knelt down in the road and, with hands joined and eyes raised to heaven, had begged Our Lady of Fàtima that she might find me alive, and at the same time also made her a promise.

"Rapidly examining my condition, I saw that my leg was broken in two places. One extremity of the broken tibia had perforated the muscles, the skin, my drawers, my trousers, and my leather leggings; and I could see the bone. The hemorrhage had been considerable; if I had lost consciousness, it would have caused death. My right hand was badly bruised and caused me intense pain at the least effort to move. The suffering in the clavicle and the arm told of numerous fractures. The blood was flowing freely from my right eye, which I thought was lost.

"When some women came up groaning and crying, I begged them to do as I should tell them. One of them had a pail with a little water in it. With my left hand, I washed my right eye, from which I thought the blood was flowing, but found the sight intact. I then made them tie a handkerchief around my head, where the blood actually was flowing from a cut about five inches long and down to the very bone. I begged the women to straighten my broken leg and to bind it with an apron in place of a bandage so as to slow up the bleeding which I sought to stop by pressing my left hand against the femoral artery.

"Meanwhile, my wife arrived with some friends and they brought me in a car — not without excruciating pain — to my office where, an hour after the accident, a first disinfection was made and temporary bandages were applied.

"I then asked to see Father Oliveira do Conde, so that he might hear my confession and bring me Holy Viaticum immediately after midnight. I began my confession by saying: 'I do not know whether after half an hour I shall still be alive. . . .'

"I was brought by rail to the hospital of the University of Coimbra, where at one o'clock in the afternoon, after a radiograph, I was given the final dressing.

"One of the fragments of the tibia had remained in contact with the rather dirty apron used for the first dressing, and from the head wound the doctors extracted pieces of stone and sand. Despite that and contrary to what usually happens in far less serious cases, there was not the least infection and I had no fever.

"One cannot impartially and honestly explain or even understand what had happened, from the point of view of mere science. It is a case so extraordinary, so exceptional, a coincidence so providential, that I cannot refrain from calling it a *miracle*.

"Besides the reasons given, there is another even stronger and more convincing, but not destined for publicity, because it is too intimate.

"I, who judged myself happy to keep my life, even *minus* a leg, now see myself whole and hearty, not at all lame, able to lead a normal life and to bring up my children.

"God grant that the memory of that great miracle may remain deeply graven in my soul.

"ACACIO DA SILVA RIBEIRO, 13 September 1927."

A FEW WOMEN

Last Stage of Tuberculosis (1922)

Thérèse de Jésus Martins, aged nineteen, was married and residing at Lisbon. In March, 1922, three months after her marriage, she began to spit out quantities of blood. After some time she was sent to the hospital, where, through the indiscretion of an employee, she discovered her real state — consumption in the final degree. At this last stage, she wished to be brought home to die, as she said, in her mother's arms. She recommended herself to the Virgin of Fàtima, promising to go there on pilgrimage and, as far as she could, on her knees. Each day she noticed that the pains disappeared for a little while and that she felt better. The hemorrhages and the fever gradually diminished, and in a week both had stopped. Three weeks later, after she had taken the last drop of the small quantity of Fàtima water she possessed, all the pains had definitely disappeared together with all the symptoms of her terrible disease.

In October she could return to Lisbon, where her physician Dr. Fernandès declared her return to health quite inexplicable.

Multiplied Tumors and Ulcer (October 13, 1928)

Mrs. Margarida Maria Lopès, of a well-known family of Lousada, suffered for ten years from a sickness which had caused five hundred tumors. "She seemed to be covered from head to foot with cork," said her physician. At the same time, an ulcer had been formed in the stomach which resisted the care of the most celebrated doctors of Porto. The patient went on pilgrimage to Fàtima, on October 13, 1928, and was instantly cured while receiving the Benediction of the Blessed Sacrament. On the twentieth of November, Dr. Mendès de Carvalho declared that his patient "bore no trace of the sicknesses from which she had been suffering."

Tumor of the Brain and Phthisis (January, 1929)

Maria José dos Santos Nunès, twenty-eight years old and residing in Lisbon, had shown the first signs of pulmonary tuberculosis in 1914. Despite the best care, her sickness progressed and in 1925 was aggravated by intestinal complications. In January, 1929, there were additional grave cerebral complications.

A famous specialist, Dr. Egas Moniz, was called in and declared that the condition of the patient was very bad and that there was nothing he could do. After his visit, he spoke plainly to a friend: "She has a tumor on the brain. In a few days the poor girl will have a terrible death. Only a miracle could save her."

Two days later a crisis occurred, lasting four full hours and causing fearful pains and convulsions. The assisting physician told the family that if this condition persisted, it would be better, out of pity for the poor sick girl, to ask God to send death as soon as possible.

At this declaration, the poor relatives turned to the Virgin of Fàtima. They moistened strips of cloth in the miraculous water

and applied them to her head. At this she regained consciousness
and remained in this condition for two days. Then she made a vow
to go to Fàtima, on a thanksgiving pilgrimage, if her prayers were
heard.

"About half-past ten," she says, "I felt a confidence such as had
never come to me in my life. I called my sister, my indefatigable
nurse, and asked her to say the beads to Our Lady of Fàtima with
me. Before beginning, I said with intense faith: 'O my Most Holy
Mother, help me, cure me of my sickness!' At the same time I took
a mouthful of Fàtima water.

"Impossible to say what I felt at that moment! A great, long cry
escaped from me. Then, smiling at those about me, I said: 'Do not
weep. Our Blessed Lady has heard me. I am not suffering at all.
I am cured!' My cry had been an exclamation of relief. Rising to
my knees in bed, I made a fervent act of thanksgiving."

And the attending physician writes: "Convinced that the patient
could not live and that I could do nothing to help her, I came back
only eight days later. The health of this lady, even before her last
infirmity, had been most feeble; now, however, I found it in a most
promising condition. She had recovered the use of all her faculties;
the change was most evident in the organs of respiration."

A GROUP OF CHILDREN

The Blessed Virgin is a mother, and what a mother! Her heart
understands, better than any other, the anguish of a mother who
fears to lose her beloved child.

Meningitis (November, 1924)

Jeannin da Costa Ferreira became very sick at the age of four.
In November, 1924, alarming symptoms were manifested: the child
lost sight and speech, fell into a lethargy, and lay as if dead. The
doctor declared it to be a very bad case of cerebrospinal meningitis
and said he thought the end was near. At this humanly hopeless
moment the sorrowing parents received the visit of a friend of the
family who brought them a little bottle of water from Fàtima. They
put some on the head of the dying child.

Twenty-four hours later the child gave signs of life. Called back suddenly, the doctor who thought him dead was much surprised and declared that the child was saved and free from any lesion.

Bronchopneumonia (March, 1928)

Gumerzindo da Silva, a baby of eighteen months, was so violently affected with bronchopneumonia on March 29, 1928, that the doctor lost all hope of saving him. Nevertheless, he remained all day beside the little fellow, trying to wrest him from death. About seven in the evening he went away, saying: "There is nothing more that can be done."

In fact, the little baby was in its death agony. Its tiny body had lost all vital warmth.

The Angelus sounded at the near-by church, and the poor mother thought it was the death knell of her little son.

"Lord," she cried, "save my child!"

At this moment (was it the answer of her prayer?) an idea came to her: "The Fàtima water!" A few hours before, the baby's godmother had brought a bottle of it and left it beside his bed. In the general consternation it had been entirely forgotten.

The mother took the bottle, nervously wet two fingers, and passed them over the cold lips of the infant. The little one opened his eyes, to the surprise of the assistants. Moved by an intense faith, the mother bathed the forehead and the face of the child. At that touch, slowly, very slowly, the vital warmth returned. A few minutes later, the little patient recovered all his faculties and began to talk as if nothing had happened. Then they called the doctor, who exclaimed: "What a transformation has taken place in my little patient!" He returned the next day to pronounce that the bronchopneumonia had completely disappeared, but he could not explain the "resurrection."

Blind and Mute (October 13, 1928)

On that day, a poor woman stood at the Cova da Iria, near the miraculous source, with her blind and mute little girl. Suddenly the child called out: "Mamma!" and, taking in her hand the medal of

Our Lady of Fàtima which she wore around her neck, she contemplated it with astonishment for the first time in her life.

Impossible to describe the joy of that mother. She was almost beside herself, kissing over and over again the dear little girl upon whom such a wonderful miracle had been wrought. The enthusiasm of the people who usually crowd about the fountain was no less great. They pressed around to see and touch the happy child. One spectator got the idea of raising the little girl to show her to the people, thus saving her from the danger of being stifled by the rejoicing crowd.

ONE LAST CASE

Finally, here is a cure taken from one of the more recent numbers of *La Voz da Fàtima*. It is an abridgment of the sworn account of the patient.

Mrs. Dulce Moreira de Sà, aged fifty-five and an inhabitant of Porto, had suffered from the age of sixteen with inflammation of the left ear, which finally deprived her of the sense of hearing in that ear. In 1935, after many useless treatments, an operation was advised. It succeeded normally; but after a few days she could no longer move her head.

She took two months of absolute rest, whose only result was more complications: vertigo, weakness of the eyes, and terrible pains in the left side of the head. During the following years she went in for innumerable consultations, treatments, and analyses — all useless. She seemed only to suffer more. Doctors gave her up. She felt an intense desire to go to Fàtima, but the doctors opposed it, because of the difficulty of moving her.

In October, 1939, she insisted upon going with her husband, who refused and only allowed her to follow the pilgrimage by radio. As May, 1940, drew near, she begged her physician again to let her go. "But how can you be carried over there? One can scarcely touch you in bed."

She answered that Our Lady was calling her; that she was ready for everything, even to die. Finally, she set out on the tenth of May, in an ambulance. It was a most painful trip. She spent one night at the hospital of Coimbra University, and the following evening reached the hospital of Fàtima sanctuary. On the morning of the thirteenth she went to Holy Communion and then heard the Mass for the sick. What followed, she tells in these few words:

"When the Blessed Sacrament passed before me where I was lying on my stretcher, it stopped for an instant. I then felt a great will to rise and I did so, without help from anyone, I was so sure I was cured."

Her husband cried out with joy and threw himself on his knees to thank God. Seated on a little cart, she rode back to the hospital, ate normally, and could bear the light of day.

She returned by car to Porto, feeling neither weakness nor vertigo, and has enjoyed a normal life since that time.

It would be easy to recount many more no less surprising cures. Here we have related a sufficient number to show the motherly kindness of Our Lady of Fàtima.

22

MORAL MIRACLES

Mary sometimes cures the body, but she more often cures the soul. There are invisible miracles, produced in the secrecy of the heart, the conscience, or the reason. Marvels of grace in the spiritual order are infinitely varied, but they blossom in the soul and are perceptible only to those in whose favor they are wrought. They are published, if at all, to only a few.

At Fàtima, our Lady multiplies them to profusion. But who could discover them in the secrecy of hearts? "If confessionals could only speak!" exclaimed one fervent apostle of Our Lady of Fàtima.

Sometimes, though, the grace of conversion is outwardly apparent. At the Cova da Iria these conversions are far more frequent and more admirable than the physical miracles.

During one pilgrimage the imposing candlelight procession was winding its way through the crowd. A group of gentlemen, there evidently for the sole purpose of seeing and being seen, were standing and enjoying the view, their hats on their heads, an air of mockery on their faces.

Suddenly, one of them, touched by grace, bared his head, fell to his knees, and began to pray.

"Oh! Are you praying too?" mocked one of his companions.

"Yes. Here, my boy, one learns to pray." And he continued undisturbed.

Not Even Baptized

On May 13, 1930, a priest who had been hearing confessions for many hours saw a man approaching whose awkward manner marked him out as one little used to confessionals.

"What do you want?" asked the priest.

"Father, I would like you to hear my confession, to give me Holy Communion and baptism." Just in that order!

He then explained that he was a merchant in Lisbon, that he had come to Fàtima for a holiday, but that, on seeing the faith of the place and the devotion to the Blessed Sacrament and to the Mother of God, he had felt a great desire to become a good Christian like the others.

The merchant prepared himself very well for baptism and for the other sacraments, which he received with the most edifying piety.

A Happy Family

There was a family of the diocese of Coimbra: father, mother, a boy, and two girls. The parents had not been to confession since the day of their marriage, seventeen years before. The father, a man with no principles and of a violent character, "did not want," he said, "any priest to put his nose into their affairs." He had allowed his children to be baptized and to make their First Communion, but nothing more. On the other hand, cursing, swearing, beating his wife and children were the order of the day. It was a real hell.

The son, Emmanuel, grew up in this school. He began by answering back, rudely, violently. Finally, one day when his father beat him, he got hold of the stick and treated him in the same way. Hence, a violent hatred arose between father and son and lasted two or three years. They would not speak to or even look at one another.

Then the father — Antonio let us call him — fell very ill. His wife, seeing that he was dying, turned to our Lady and promised to go on foot to Fàtima if he recovered.

He did recover; but when his wife said she would go to Fàtima to keep her promise, he answered dryly: "Why did you make that promise? You won't go to Fàtima! I don't believe in those mummeries!"

A few days later, however, his wife met a good friend of hers who told her she was going to Fàtima with her family and invited her to go along.

"I can't go. My husband won't hear of it. But you come this evening and ask him."

That evening the friend came. "Antonio, tomorrow we're going to Fàtima. I'm preparing the provisions today." And she detailed the next day's menu. "You, too, should come, Antonio."

"I go? But, Madam, you're dreaming."

"Well, let your wife and daughters come."

Not to be too rude, he consented. His wife and the two girls had prepared the basket that night and were ready for bed, when Antonio said: "Listen. I'm going there too. I want to see what mummeries you're going to do."

"Oh, Holy Virgin. Thanks!" the good woman was about to exclaim, but she refrained and interiorly thanked our Lady for beginning to touch her husband's heart.

The trip was very long and, when they came to a steep mountain ascent, Antonio lost all patience. He began a litany of imprecations that seemed endless. His wife, utterly ashamed, invoked the Blessed Virgin, while trying to calm him down — without any success, however, until they actually reached the sanctuary.

"What are all those people doing? What is this?" Antonio exclaimed.

"It is Our Lady of Fàtima. We have arrived at last, and we shall assist at the procession. You'll see how beautiful it is."

But they had barely entered the sanctuary, when he suddenly fainted away. The Servites brought him in their arms to the hospital, where two physicians tried every means to bring about his recovery. He seemed dead.

"What a misfortune! He will die without receiving the sacraments! And it is seventeen years since he went to confession!" his wife exclaimed, continuing to moan and to invoke the protection of all the saints, all the while making her husband's public confession.

Finally she and her daughters were induced to withdraw, while a Servite sat up to watch the invalid. Soon after she perceived a slight movement in his body. Then he straightened out violently.

"It is death," said the nurse to herself. But he opened his eyes
and looked about him, as though afraid.

"Where am I?"

"At Fàtima, at our Lady's hospital. Wait a minute, I shall get
you something hot to drink. It is nearly midnight, and you surely
want to go to Holy Communion tomorrow, don't you?" said the
Servite, feigning to ignore his real dispositions.

"I? Perhaps . . . but I haven't been to confession."

"Well, don't bother about that. I'll get you a confessor. One
expressly for you. You'll see how much you'll like him."

And she hurried out . . . to meet the wife, still complaining of
the sad lot of her family. "Don't cry, my good woman, your husband
is going to confession in a few minutes."

"Don't make fun of me, my dear."

"It's the truth." And she told her briefly what had happened.

Now the wife was crying, not for sorrow but for joy, and blessing
our Lady. Suddenly, she added: "Ah, if my son Emmanuel, who has
been fighting him for so many years, could only go to confession
too!"

"Today, at Fàtima, everybody goes to confession. Go and get
him, and come here all together."

While the wife was hunting for her son in the crowds, the priest
arrived to hear Antonio's confession, made with the most excellent
dispositions.

By this time the boy had turned up.

"Emmanuel, your father is going to confession. You must go too,
so that you may go to Communion tomorrow with him."

"My father is going to confession now?"

"Yes, just now; the priest is still there."

"Then, if you want me to, I'll go!"

After confession, he looked like a lamb. "Papa," he said, "don't
be angry with me any more! Forgive me everything!"

With tears in his eyes, the father answered: "Come here,
Emmanuel. It's you that has to forgive me. I've been dreadfully
mean to you."

Grace and divine benedictions came down upon that family,
through Mary's intercession. The next morning they all went to

Communion together, for the first time, and joyfully assisted at all the ceremonies.

Indeed, they were loath to leave that holy spot. So much so that, the next month they were all there again to thank the Blessed Virgin for the happiness they had never known before, and also to show their gratitude to the Servite who had been the instrument of Mary's mercy.

"And at the Hour of Our Death"

For how many souls coming impenitent to the gates of eternity has Fàtima been the Key of Paradise! Here are a few examples.

Marius dos Santos, aged thirty-five and living at Porto, was dying of tuberculosis, but would not go to confession, or even, as he said, "see the shadow of a priest." A pious lady, wishing to save this poor soul, had promised at Fàtima on the thirteenth of February, that if the patient asked spontaneously for a priest she would publish it as a miracle. On the morning of the twentieth, the sick man asked for a confessor, without anyone having said a word, confessed himself, and received Viaticum, weeping for sorrow and for joy. Three days later he died in the same excellent dispositions.

The vice-rector of the College of Bahia wrote the following: "In October, 1928, an old man, the grandfather of three of our pupils, had been admitted to the Portuguese hospital. It was Sunday and we were making a novena in our chapel to Our Lady of Fàtima. The preacher spoke of the efficacy of Mary's intercession to obtain the grace of the last sacraments for the dying. In the middle of the sermon, the oldest of the three grandsons came up to me and asked for a medal of Our Lady of Fàtima to give to his grandfather, who, though dangerously ill, would not receive the sacraments. I gave it to him, and the child left immediately. After the sermon, I asked everybody to pray that the preacher's words might be realized in the present instance. Half an hour afterward a telephone call from the hospital informed us that the sick man, on seeing a priest, his friend who had come to visit him, had asked to receive the sacraments. A few minutes later he had breathed his last, *"in osculo Domini."*

Let us note also the account in *La Voz da Fàtima* for November 13, 1935, according to which the conversion of Queen Astrid of Belgium was obtained through the intercession of Our Lady of Fàtima.

Miracles of the body, miracles of the soul — which of the two better demonstrates the power and the goodness of Mary? To send away the paralytic cured, or out of Saul the Pharisee to make Paul the Apostle of the Gentiles — which is the greater prodigy? Is it not the second? But for these miracles there is no *Bureau of Authentication.* They are inscribed only in the *Book of Life.*

23

"THE GREATER MIRACLE"

There are individual conversions, some of them hard to obtain. There are also collective conversions — the return to religion of families, communities, and villages — still more rare and more difficult to secure. But who can compute the abundance of grace required for the conversion, the upraising of a whole people, a complete nation? This miracle of miracles, we can say without hesitation, Our Lady of Fàtima accomplished, in the twentieth century, in favor of Portugal.

BEFORE 1917

In the eighteenth century the great splendor of Portugal began to diminish. Since the discovery of the New World, Portugal ruled the sea, had built itself a rich empire, and had planted the cross in many distant lands. Her decline coincided with the growth of masonic influence in the government.

With the invasion of Napoleon, the ideas of the French Revolution penetrated Portugal. King John VI was forced to seek refuge in his colony in Brazil, and his absence did not contribute to the preservation of order. Finally, to drive the French out of the peninsula, the English landed in the country and remained there till John VI returned in 1820.

John VI had two sons, Dom Pedro, self-proclaimed emperor of Brazil, and Dom Miguel, who succeeded him as king of Portugal. War broke out between the two. Dom Pedro seized the power, after promising to introduce "a new order." The clergy suffered, religious communities were banished from the country, and relations with the Holy See were interrupted. This condition persisted until 1842, when it was followed by a religious restoration. The Church remained relatively free until the end of the century.

Unfortunately the press was mainly masonic and the working classes were drawn into masonic organizations. In 1901 there was a sectarian movement which victimized the religious communities in particular. During this time, the monarchy was so weak that it prepared its own overthrow. There were not more than ten thousand agitators in the country, yet they assassinated the king and threw the country into revolution.

Despite all this, the people remained fundamentally Christian and attached to traditional religious practices, with the exception perhaps of the workers in large cities. As in France at this same time, the government did not represent the true popular opinion but that of an organized tyrannical minority. The result was anarchy, with its cortege of misery and ruin. From 1910 to 1926 there were sixteen violent revolutions and forty-three changes of ministry, a real chaos. Freedom of worship was impeded, apostolic and charitable works were rendered impossible. Religious orders were suppressed; the number of clerical students was slowly diminishing; the clergy were everywhere impoverished and insufficient in number, and the Catholic press was reduced to a few provincial weeklies, without weight or influence.

In March, 1916, as a climax, the government allowed itself to be drawn into the war. But the finances of the country could not bear this new burden; it spelled ruin and bankruptcy.

AFTER 1917

Suddenly, in the winter of 1917–1918, Portugal gave signs of pacification and recovery.

On October 28, 1917, *O Seculo,* a once antireligious newspaper, dared to publish the Viscount de Montelo's protestation, issued in the name of the Catholics of Santarem against the sacrilegious attack on the Cova da Iria and the burlesque manifestation at Santarem. Times were certainly changing!

On the eighth of December, the first Feast of the Immaculate

Conception after the apparitions, Sidonio Pais seized power and inaugurated a policy of reparation. Some bishops were recalled from banishment. At the same time certain particularly odious legislations were annulled.

In February, 1918, when the Portuguese bishops held a meeting in Lisbon, they already could write to Pope Benedict XV that the position of the Church in Portugal had been somewhat bettered. The situation continued to improve, and diplomatic relations with the Holy See were re-established by the nomination of a nuncio at Lisbon and a Portuguese minister at Rome.

In December, 1918, Pais was assassinated and political struggles began anew. But Catholics were strengthened by the events at Fàtima and dared to organize for resistance. Even before the creation of Catholic Action by Pius XI, numerous associations of social apostolate had begun to arise.

In 1926, the Portuguese episcopate held its first national council in modern times. And it was on the twenty-eighth of May of that same year, that Marshal Gomès da Costa, with General Carmona and General Cabeçadas, established a military triumvirate, and drove the freemasons from power. Two years later, the ministry of finance was occupied by that great Catholic leader, M. Oliveira Salazar, professor of law at the University of Coimbra. Since then, this "plain-clothes dictator" has governed the once much troubled country in peace and order.

THE ANTI-COMMUNIST VOW

In 1936 the terrible revolution in Spain occurred and plunged that country into an ordeal of fire and blood. Nothing was to be feared more than the spread of the contagion from one neighboring land to the other. Yet during this entire storm, international Communism never succeeded in seriously troubling the political and social life of the Portuguese nation even for one day.

Some weeks before the cataclysm broke out in Spain, that is in May, 1936, during their annual retreat at the Cova da Iria, all the bishops of Portugal collectively promised the Virgin of Fàtima to organize an extraordinary national pilgrimage, in May, 1938, in order to consecrate the whole country to her Immaculate Heart, if she would deign to preserve the "Land of Holy Mary" from the threat of godless Communism.

Two months after this vow, the Communist revolution broke out in Spain, with its monstrous program: extermination of the secular and regular clergy, implacable suppression of all the elements of order, complete annihilation of the Catholic religion and even of all that might recall it in the public and private treasures of history, art, and science.

Massacres, calamities, and ruin were accumulated by the Communists in Spain. Yet all this time, despite the efforts of international godlessness, peace and order reigned in Portugal, allowing the country to pursue tranquilly its conquest of material prosperity and moral progress.

The vow of 1936 had to be fulfilled. The episcopate and the people did so most worthily. One can say that on May 13, 1938, the whole nation took up the pilgrim's staff and came humbly to the feet of Our Lady of Fàtima to offer its homage of deepest gratitude.

Twenty archbishops and bishops, surrounding Cardinal Cerejeira, patriarch of Lisbon, and half a million faithful — one out of every twelve inhabitants — renewed their consecration and that of the country to the Immaculate Heart of Mary in her blessed sanctuary.

That same day, throughout the whole country, hundreds of thousands of people, in union with the pilgrims, and forming one heart and one soul with them, offered in their respective churches the same homage of love, gratitude, and faithfulness to the Most Blessed Virgin.

AND NOW

It is impossible to give a complete account here of the religious and civil condition of Portugal by 1941. Suffice it to show, in a few brief lines, the exceptional character of the situation.

First there was the signing, right in the middle of the European war (June 1, 1940), of doubtless the most perfect concordat ever signed by the Vatican, which promises to Portugal a long period of civil peace and social and religious progress.

The concordat was completed by a missionary agreement, which may be considered an initiative worthy of imitation in matters of international law.

Such an act was above all a triumph. People, it is said, have the government — and the laws — they deserve. It was the profoundly religious life of the Portuguese people that made such an accord as necessary as it was natural.

This religious vitality is most striking yet today. Faith is everywhere professed, openly and proudly. The sacraments are honored by all classes of society. The First Friday and Saturday and the thirteenth of each month are regular Communion days for a considerable and ever growing number of the faithful.

Catholic Action was officially organized in 1933, and by 1940 it already numbered 2300 sections, grouping together 55,000 persons. These frame the immense crowd of Fàtima Crusaders, who are more than half a million.

One of the happiest symptoms of religious growth is the considerable increase in religious vocations. In 1910 all male and female religious were banished from the country. By 1918 they had begun to return. In 1934 the *Catholic Theological Dictionary* gave the total number of 370 religious priests for the whole country. By 1941 the priests of the Society of Jesus alone had attained to almost that number. In eight years the total number had multiplied four times.

For feminine religious communities let us take for example only the Dorothy Sisters, to which Lucy of Jesus belongs. In 1917 they had only the Asilo de Vilar, which they were able to keep open by secularizing and appearing like lay teachers. In 1934, on the contrary, the *Annual* for this congregation listed fifteen large establishments: boardinghouses, schools, orphanages, and even one university college. Since that date many more foundations have been made.

The Catholic press could not but progress greatly in such a *milieu*. The Lisbon daily, *Novidades*, honors it especially, and *La Voz da Fàtima* runs to 350,000 copies monthly.

What a marvel to find this land of peace and prosperity in a devastated, war-torn Europe. With 26.7 per 1000 inhabitants, Portugal holds the second rank in Europe for its proportion of births. It is prospering financially, and is the only country in Europe where, in the year 1941, food rationing was unknown. For fourteen years, it has enjoyed such continuity of government and such political peace that it has not seen the overthrow of even one ministry.

THE CAUSE?

Many studies on Portugal speak of the spiritual, moral, and material restoration of the country, but not a word of Fàtima. For any fair mind, the evidence loudly proclaims the cause of this transformation; what is called "the Portuguese Experience" cannot be understood without Fàtima.

How is it that the whole religious and national life of the country has been changed in less than one generation? How is it that Catholicism, once persecuted, has flowered as it had not for centuries? How is it that the spirit of Catholicism impregnates and dominates the whole of its social, economic, and political life? Why has Portugal suddenly stopped in its descent toward the abyss, and now walks calmly, peacefully, toward the re-establishment of its ancient splendor? Why, we ask, is a country in which revolution had become habitual now marked by a stable government? Why is this country one of those rare ones in all Europe in which order and liberty are closely mated? Why, in fact, is Portugal one of the only countries to be preserved for twenty-five years from both civil and foreign war? All these are enigmas to be solved.

We are persuaded that neither Mr. Salazar nor their Excellencies, the bishops of Portugal, will gainsay us if we call this double religious and national "miracle" a true miracle of divine omnipotence, obtained by the mercy and goodness of Our Lady of Fàtima.

Without Fàtima, Salazar would not have been possible. He would not have been called to the government. He would not have come to the first rank of power, nor would he have remained there. Certainly he built up the country's finances — by crushing it at first with taxes. Why did the country accept this heavy burden, though at times groaning under it, if not because, thanks to Fàtima, the atmosphere had become more Christian, men's ideas had become pacific, passions were calmed and souls had changed?

Salazar put order in the political and social domain; but it was by crushing down the elements of disorder, which previously had always triumphed. He did it without violence, without demonstrations of strength. Why was that? Because *now*, the whole country was ready to stand behind him.

Besides, would Salazar be the chief he is, if he were not the austere, pious Catholic we know him to be? One of his compatriots has said: "He, too, bears his cross." And a Frenchman added: "He is possessed of a great certitude, and it comes to Salazar from his Catholicism." In his faith, therefore, lies the secret of his strength.

Recently celebrating the double centenary of the foundation and independence of Portugal, Pius XII made an express allusion to the divine help brought to this country by the Virgin of Fàtima.

"God will bless," he said, "the chivalrous people of Portugal, whom Our Lady of Fàtima protects, the Blessed Virgin of the Rosary who obtained the victory of Lepanto."

In the collective pastoral of 1942, written to celebrate the jubilee feasts of Fàtima, the episcopate affirmed that the prodigious renewal of Portugal was caused by the apparitions of Our Lady of Fàtima in 1917.

"Is there even one truly Catholic Portuguese who does not recognize that our privileged situation is a reflection of that light brought to Fàtima by our Lady, projected by her upon the souls of the three little shepherds, and by their means upon the whole world? But it is not even necessary to have faith in order to admit this fact. It is only necessary to see how extraordinary is our position, in order to recognize that a higher power is extended above us, and that a tender and merciful Heart watches lovingly over Portugal! . . .

"One who would have closed his eyes twenty-five years ago, and would open them now, would no longer recognize Portugal, so deep and so extensive is the transformation wrought by that humble, invisible factor which we know as the apparitions of Fàtima."

Our Lady of the Rosary came down from heaven upon the blessed mountain of Fàtima; then, like God's messenger, she knocked at the door of every home in Portugal. Very rare are the families where the old custom of the daily beads has not been revived. The picture of Our Lady of Fàtima is honored everywhere. And we know that wherever Mary enters, Jesus comes with her.

From this widespread, national love for the Queen of Heaven and her divine Son is derived that admirable social and political concord which, with the added blessing of heaven, constitutes the entire secret of the particularly privileged position of Portugal.

If Portugal is an example for the other nations, these must not forget that it is also a miracle of God's grace. None will succeed in the political, economic, and social "experience" of this country, without imitating also the depth of its religion and its devotion to the Queen of Angels and of men. Blessed the people whose true king is the Lord and of whom Mary is truly the queen.

The message of mercy on the part of Our Lady of Fàtima was not intended for Portugal alone, any more than the message of Lourdes had been meant for France alone. And here precisely attention may be called to a remarkable coincidence. It was on April 16, 1917, that Lenin and Trotzky arrived at Petrograd and in the following days headed the Bolshevist revolution, which no later than November 7 of the same year triumphed at Petrograd and a few days later at Moscow. Its set purpose was not the subduing of Russia alone but of the entire world by fire and blood.

Note that precisely between the two dates mentioned here all the apparitions of Our Lady of Fàtima took place. While Anti-Christ unchained the most frightful wars, not merely against true religion but against the very idea of God, and against civil society, at that very period Mary appeared, the great, undying enemy of the infernal serpent, disclosing to the world her Immaculate Heart, revealing the sure way of salvation, urging us to do penance and to flee sin, especially the sin of impurity and the improprieties of fashion, and on the other hand recommending insistently the daily devout recitation of the rosary as the key to the divine treasure house.

24

CONCLUSION: THE MESSAGE OF FÀTIMA

RETURN TO THE GOSPEL

In the "mystery" of Fàtima, there are two things to be considered: the prodigies and the message. The prodigies strike one first: they are unequaled in history. But what must be remembered above all is the message, for which the prodigies were but the orchestration.

Since the tenderness of her maternal heart prompted Mary even to come down from heaven, amid so wonderful a profusion of proofs and miracles, in order that she might tell her children what the good Lord asked of them, it is very evident that she desires to see Christians pay great attention to the content of her message. Is it necessary to say that it must interest not only the Portuguese, but Catholics the whole world over?

With the death of John, the last apostle, the divine work of revelation for the whole Church was closed. The private revelations made by God to a few privileged souls could add nothing to the deposit of faith confided to the Church. To the shepherds of Aljustrel, Mary would not teach a new doctrine. By their intervention, she meant only to recall to a world that was forgetting it, the eternal message of her Son.

Each of her actions, each of her words at Fàtima, is like an echo of the main maxims of the Gospel, the most urgent, doubtless, for the modern world.

The essential evil from which it suffers is the forgetfulness of the eternal truths: we live, more and more, *in* the passing moment and *for* the passing moment. Now, if the Gospel could revolutionize the world, it was because its message was essentially an explosion of eternal truth amid the Jewish and pagan worldliness. From this point of view, the main word of the Saviour is: *Quid prodest?* "What doth it profit a man if he gain the whole world and suffer the loss of his soul?"

Mary knew it was most opportune to recall this truth in our times, when the things of eternity hold not the slightest place in the press, in conversations, in current literature, and consequently in the real interests of Christians.

The Virgin of Fàtima came in a motherly way, as she had done at Lourdes, to recall to her overbusy children their true destiny.

She spoke to the little shepherds, not of their flocks or of their earthly future, but of heaven, of their salvation, of the salvation of their dead companions, of the eternal lot of sinners.

To give them a foretaste of heaven, to which she invited them, she gave them, even at the first apparition, the sensation of the divine presence by means of that mysterious light which penetrated to the very depths of their soul. And we know the profound impression the children retained of this.

The terrible vision of hell, at the third apparition, can well inspire us with pity for those poor souls whom sin draws toward that abyss of fire, and also give us a salutary fear of divine chastisement.

That same day, she taught them, and teaches us, a short and altogether simple prayer. Every word recalls our last end here and what is to follow it. Repeated many times a day, it can but anchor those great realities deeply in our souls and lead to serious resolutions. Mary uses with us the method of Ignatius of Loyola in repeating to Francis Xavier, until it brought about the perfect conversion of his friend: "What does it profit a man . . . ?"

By rapidly calling two of the little seers to her throne in heaven, Mary shows us how small a price she puts on the goods of this world for those she loves. In this way she repeats to us what she said to Bernadette: "I will make you happy, not in this world, but in the next."

Heaven must be the great thought of Christians, as it was of Francis and Jacinta, and they will win it by being "like little children." "Whosoever, therefore, shall humble himself as this little child, he is the greater in the kingdom of heaven."

Another characteristic of the good news of Jesus is the call to union with God, the invitation to constant prayer: "Without Me, you can do nothing." "Ask and you shall receive." "Pray always and never cease."

The time consecrated to God in prayer is more and more reduced and minimized for Christians of our day. Worldly preoccupations, business, and modern agitation turn us from God, bend us to earth — of which we would make a paradise — and lead us fatally to sin.

The marvels of Fàtima are directed by the mercy of our heavenly Mother to turn our thoughts to heaven and to God. Let us read again her words to the little seers, and remember with what fervor those children devoted themselves to prayer and sacrifice for the love of Jesus. As soon as their little souls beheld the vision, their only desire was to please Jesus, to love Him and His Immaculate Mother.

Fàtima is the reward of the fervent prayer and candid love of three little children; but it is also actually the most frequented place of Catholic prayer throughout the world. Is not that both lesson and example for us?

But the message of Fàtima dwells particularly on two points: *conversion or penance* and *the recitation of the rosary*. These are the two elements in the declaration of our Lady at her last visit. She had announced from the beginning that, on that day, she would tell who she was and what she wanted. Now, a few moments before the great prodigy which was to add a divine signature to her words, she declared:

"I am the Lady of the Rosary. Men must amend their lives and ask pardon for their sins. They must not continue to offend our Lord who is already so deeply offended."

"Continue," was her admonition, "to recite the rosary every day."

"IF YOU DO NOT PENANCE . . ."

The three synoptical Gospels say that the Saviour began by preaching penance (in Greek *metanoian,* that is, conversion).

Penance, in the sense of the Gospels and theology, is an act of justice by which the sinner, recalling with sorrow and confusion that he has offended God, tries to repair this outrage and regain divine grace.

"Do penance, for the kingdom of heaven is at hand." "Except you do penance, you shall all likewise perish," said the Lord. His own Mother could speak no other language, especially in our day. Because men were breaking away more and more from divine law, sin redoubled its violence on earth. It seemed as if her Immaculate Heart was preoccupied with but one thing: to turn men away from the paths of sin and bring them to battle with all their strength against this terrible enemy of their happiness and their salvation.

At Lourdes the Mother of Mercy cried out: "Penance! Penance!" At Fàtima, she repeats the same call. She came especially for that.

The very word *sin* is almost forgotten on the lips of men and its very notion clouded; morality has hardly any other rule than free caprice, personal interest, or pleasure. Mary wished to reawaken a sense of sin, to inspire a profound horror for it, and to show us its dangers. How often at Fàtima that word dropped from her lips!

We have read her formal declaration: "Men must amend their lives and ask pardon for their sins. They must not continue to offend our Lord, already so deeply offended." It is truly the Gospel of the *metanoian*.

In her notebook, Sister Mary of the Dolors adds these remarks, addressed to everyone: "In this apparition, the words which remained most deeply impressed in my heart were those by which our holy Mother in heaven begged men not to continue to offend our Lord, already so deeply offended. What a loving complaint and what supplication they contain! Oh, how I wish they would sound throughout the world, and that all the children of our heavenly Mother would hear her voice!"

The counsels of Mary were accompanied by a promise, a magnificent promise. Conversion is the first condition of eternal salvation for each individual child of God; but it will also have its reward here below: "If men amend their lives, the war will soon cease."

At her first visit, Mary asked the children to make sacrifices, to offer themselves as victims for the reparation of sins and for the conversion of sinners.

In the third apparition especially, she showed her little confidants
the sad consequences of sin — here below, the war, synthesis of all
evils; in the other world, the flames of hell. The prayer she taught
them that day to say after each decade of the beads begins with
the petition: *"My Jesus, forgive us our sins. . . ."*

On the nineteenth of August particularly, Mary touched the
hearts of her little friends: *"Pray and make sacrifices for sinners, for
many souls go to hell because there are none to make sacrifices and
to pray for them."*

Thus, in all the conversations of the Lady with the little shepherds, she taught them to use the two great weapons of prayer and
penance against sin; to receive with courage all sufferings sent by
God; to offer voluntary sacrifices, and to pray many rosaries. All
that must be used for the conversion of sinners or at least to expiate
their faults and repair the sorrow they cause the Sacred Heart of
Jesus and the Immaculate Heart of Mary.

On this subject, one should also consider the words of our Lady
to the dying Jacinta: "The sins which lead most souls to hell are
the sins of the flesh. Luxurious living must be avoided, people must
do penance and repent of their sins. Great penance is indispensably
necessary."

By this "luxury" which must be avoided we must understand
especially the immodest fashions for which Jacinta, from her hospital bed, manifested such aversion. These are, doubtless, some of
the offenses which so greatly saddened the Immaculate Heart of
Mary and which return so often in the words of the vision and in
the prayers of the children.

It was on her hospital bed, too, that the little seer spoke of the
actual necessity of doing penance: "Our Lady said that there are
many wars and disputes in the world; but wars are only the punishment for the sins of the world. The Blessed Virgin can no longer
hold back the arm of her Son over the world. There must be amend-
ment. If men repented of their sins, our Lord would forgive them;
but if they do not change their life, the chastisement will come."

The message of Fàtima is, therefore, essentially an invitation to
penance, to real conversion.

THE ROSARY — THE WORLD'S SALVATION

Mary, at Fàtima, has closely united the spirit of penance to the recitation of the rosary. By recommending that devotion, she calls us back to the Gospels. The Our Father, which we repeat six times when we say the beads, abridges the Sermon on the Mount.

The meditation on the fifteen mysteries of the rosary epitomizes the whole economy of the Redemption (except the Saviour's public ministry), giving the faithful occasion to think over the Gospel and to practice the virtues it teaches.

What can lead us to a good life more efficaciously than meditation on the example of Jesus and His holy Mother?

That is why saints and popes have so strongly recommended this devotion. Leo XIII not only renewed the teachings of Gregory XVI and Pius IX, but he himself wrote *twelve encyclicals on the rosary.* Pius X says in his testament "The prayer of the rosary is of all prayers the most beautiful, the most rich in grace, and the one which most touches the heart of the Mother of God. . . . If you want peace to reign in your homes say the beads there, every day, with your family."

Benedict XV, as we know, wrote to all the world only a week before the first apparition, beseeching men to beg Mary's intercession through the rosary. Pius XI insisted on it even more strongly. Then came Pius XII who, in 1941, so highly praised the rosary as to call it the essential family prayer, since it answers perfectly the needs of young married people, of children, the young man, the young girl, the mother, the old people, the dying — the entire family.

At Fàtima Mary said: "I am the Lady of the Rosary," thus confirming and underlining all the teachings of the sovereign pontiffs on the importance and efficacy of the holy rosary.

Our Lady first appeared to the three children as they were saying their beads, *nor did she fail at each single visit to recommend this prayer to her little friends.*

On the thirteenth of July, five or six thousand faithful fervently recited the beads with the children. For the third time the apparition insisted on the necessity of saying the rosary, and added a particularly pressing intention for that period: "The beads are to be said in honor of our Lady, to obtain the end of the war, for she alone can come to our help."

The same demand was repeated again on the thirteenth of September. In addition she counseled the sick who sought a cure, and others who desired other graces, to recite their chaplet faithfully every day.

Finally, on the thirteenth of October, came the promised miracle seen by 70,000 people. Like the Lord on Mount Sinai, Mary at the Cova da Iria, with the help of fearful prodigies and in the midst of "the sincere contrition of souls," proclaimed the law of penance and prayer, the prayer of the rosary. "I am the Lady of the Rosary . . . Continue every day to say the beads."

We must note that our Lady, after showing herself five times to the children under the same form, had shown herself to them, this sixth and last time, under other aspects. They had seen her with St. Joseph and the Infant Jesus; then she showed herself to Lucy only under the form of Our Lady of the Seven Dolors and, finally, under the appearance of Our Lady of Mount Carmel.

Why was this? The most acceptable opinion is that, commenting on the title she had just given herself — the Lady of the Rosary — Mary wished to recall the three kinds of mysteries meditated upon in the rosary.

The sight of Mary in the midst of the Holy Family makes one think of the Joyful Mysteries which encourage us, by the example of Jesus in His hidden life, to the practice of the ordinary duties of a Christian life.

Our Lady of Dolors recalls the Sorrowful Mysteries which excite us to contrition and to penance, so much recommended in the course of the preceding apparitions.

Our Lady of Mount Carmel doubtless represented the Queen of the Glorious Mysteries. Mother of Christian hope, she wishes to draw us to perfect love of God and to the desire of heaven, like little Francis and his sister Jacinta. She delivers souls from purgatory by the scapular of Carmel and she promises to introduce into paradise the souls of those who shall have invoked her on earth like the little children of Fàtima.

Thus, this triple manifestation was a most distinct explanation of that title which Mary had given herself, Queen of the Most Holy Rosary.

It is as though the Queen of the Angels has willed to "canonize" that devotion of the rosary and recommend it to all the faithful. After the Sacrifice of the Mass and the liturgical Office, there is no more *Catholic* prayer than the holy rosary; there is none more pleasing to the Immaculate Heart of Mary; none more efficacious; and, therefore, none more necessary.

May we finally understand, in the light of the events of Fàtima, that our personal salvation and that of present-day society is to be found in a return to the maxims of the Gospel and to the rosary, piously recited in a spirit of penance.

THE IMMACULATE HEART OF MARY — OUR SWEET HOPE

His Eminence, Cardinal Cerejeira, has proclaimed that a new era is opening upon the world, that of the Immaculate Heart of Mary. For more than twenty-five years, Sister Lucy of Jesus has known that she must remain "alone" on earth because our Lord wished her to establish there "the devotion to the Immaculate Heart" of His Mother. Her little cousin Jacinta, before dying, begged her not to be unfaithful to transmitting this element of the Lady's message: "When the moment will have come, say clearly that the good Lord grants His graces through the Immaculate Heart — that we must not hesitate to ask these of her; that the Heart of Jesus desires to be honored together with the Immaculate Heart of Mary; that men ought to request the peace from the Immaculate Heart, because God has confided it to her."

Jacinta, the little shepherdess of Aljustrel, had not forgotten that the Angel of Cabeço had told them to console the heart of their heavenly Mother. She had kept in mind the words of the Lady of the Cova da Iria, bidding her little seers console her heart for the grief given it by the sins of the world; and she had remembered the Lady's promise to return in order "to ask for *the Consecration of the World to her Immaculate Heart*" and *the Communion of Reparation on the First Saturday of the month.* It was her profound love for this Immaculate Heart that kept up her courage in the cruel sufferings that caused her death.

The "moment" spoken of by Jacinta seems now to have arrived. Lately, Sister Lucy has repeatedly declared to ecclesiastical authority that Mary desires to see the world consecrate itself to her Immaculate Heart, and that the practice of Communion on the first Saturday of the month should spread.

Pope Pius XII wished to accomplish the first of these requests when, on October 31 and December 8, 1942, he solemnly consecrated the Church and the world to the Immaculate Heart of Mary. And the immense crowd, deeply moved, could well have felt that here little Jacinta's vision was realized, when in the midst of a period of war and unhappiness she beheld "the Holy Father on his knees in a great church, before the Immaculate Heart of Mary, and with him many people in prayer."

How grateful we must be to His Holiness for having accomplished the wish of our heavenly Mother! Now, may all the dioceses, all the parishes, all Christian families, all believers in the whole world, be consecrated to the Immaculate Heart of Mary. But let it be a consecration that is in truth a generous and total gift, the sign of the transformation of our lives by a sincere conversion.

This is the message brought to our troubled century by Our Lady of Fàtima. That she enforced it with so many and such great "signs from heaven" proves that it is perfectly adapted to our needs and that, if understood, it would bring to our society precisely what it lacks today.

Catholics of the twentieth century, let us not, by inattention to the visit and the words of Mary, draw upon ourselves those reproachful words of Christ to His own country: "If thou hadst known, and that in this thy day, the things that are to thy peace!"

It is the duty of those who know this message to spread it, to follow its prescriptions, and to recommend their observance to others. In particular let us recite and have others recite the rosary every day, so as to obtain by the intercession of Our Lady of the Rosary the conversion of sinners and the return of peace to this poor, stricken world.

THE CROSS QUESTIONINGS

Aljustrel, September 27

From the time of the first rumors concerning the apparitions of
Fàtima, the administrator of the patriarchate of Lisbon appointed
Manuel Nunes Formigâo* to supervise the subsequent occurrences.
The latter was personally present at the fifth apparition on the
thirteenth of September, and then returned some days later to
complete the inquiries he had begun.

On the twenty-seventh of September he presented himself for
the first time at the home of Lucy's parents. Madame dos Santos
received him kindly. Having learned the purpose of his visit, she
told him that her daughter was working in the grape harvest some
twenty minutes' distance from the house. She immediately sent
for her.

Her two cousins, Jacinta and Francis, on returning from the fields,
learned from the neighbors that a priest was awaiting them at
their aunt's house. Jacinta arrived first. Surprised by the presence
of unfamiliar people, she at first appeared to be embarrassed, and
replied in monosyllables in a voice that could scarcely be heard.
Happily, the arrival of her brother put her at ease.

Francis entered with his cap on his head. His little sister made
a sign for him to remove it, but he paid no attention to her. Then,
without further ceremony, he sat down and submitted freely and
without constraint to the examination of the visitor. In the meantime Jacinta had left the room.

---

* He signs his articles and books with the pseudonym: *Viscount de Montelo*.
His appointment was made by the administrator of the patriarchate since the
cardinal patriarch himself had been banished by the government.

The Interrogation of Francis:

"What did you see at Cova da Iria these past months?"

"I saw the Blessed Virgin."

"Where did she appear?"

"Over an evergreen oak."

"Did she appear suddenly, or did you see her come otherwise?"

"I saw her come from the direction of the sunrise; then she stopped over the evergreen oak."

"Did she come slowly or quickly?"

"She always came quickly."

"Did you hear what she said to Lucy?"

"No, I didn't hear anything."

"Did you sometimes speak to the Lady? Did she say anything to you?"

"No, I didn't ask her any questions, and she spoke only with Lucy."

"Toward whom did she look, toward the three of you or only toward Lucy?"

"Toward the three of us, but her gaze rested especially on Lucy."

"Up to now, did she weep or smile sometimes?"

"Neither the one nor the other. She is always serious."

"How was she dressed?"

"She wore a long dress. Over it there was a veil which covered her head and went down to the bottom of her dress."

"What was the color of her dress and veil?"

"It was white; and the dress was trimmed with a gold border."

"What posture did the Lady take?"

"As if praying. She held her folded hands as high as her breast."

"Did she have anything in her hand?"

"She held around the palm and the back of her hand a rosary which hung down over her dress."

"Did she have anything on her ears?"

"Her ears couldn't be seen because they were covered by her veil."

"What color were the beads of her rosary?"

"They were white too."

"Was the Lady beautiful?"

"Oh, yes!"

"More beautiful than that little girl you see over there playing in the street?"

"Much more beautiful!"

"But there are some women more beautiful than that little girl."
"She is more beautiful than anyone I have ever seen."

Interrogation of Little Jacinta:

During the interrogation of Francis, Jacinta was playing on the street with some little girls of her own age. In her turn she was called and made to sit down on a bench, and they obtained from her answers as complete and as detailed as were those of her brother.

"Did you see the Blessed Virgin on the thirteenth of each month, from the month of May until now?"
"Yes, I saw her."
"From what direction did she come?"
"She came from heaven; from the direction of the sun."
"How was she dressed?"
"She wore a white dress, trimmed with gold, and on her head there was a white veil too."
"What was the color of her hair?"
"One couldn't see it, because it was hidden by the veil."
"Did she wear earrings?"
"I don't know, because one couldn't see her ears."
"How did she hold her hands?"
"She held them folded as high as her breast, her fingers pointing up."
"Was her rosary in her right hand or in her left?"
To this question the child immediately replied: "In her right hand."
Then, when they tried to puzzle her, she became troubled and confused, not knowing too precisely which of her two hands corresponded to the one in the apparition which held the rosary.
"What did she command Lucy to do with so great earnestness?"
"To recite the rosary every day."
"And you, do you say it?"
"Yes, every day with Francis and Lucy."

The Interrogation of Lucy:

Lucy kept them waiting about half an hour. Taller and more developed than her two cousins, robust and healthy, she presented herself with a naturalness which contrasted with the timidity of Jacinta. She had been ten years old the previous March 22. Her father, Antonio dos Santos, was a good man but not very pious. Her mother, Maria Rosa, on the contrary, was a model Christian woman, entirely absorbed in bringing up her children in the fear of God and love of duty. The pious woman did not know what to think of her daughter's visions. She rather wished that the visions were true, but feared lest Lucy might be a victim of hallucination, nor did she view without anxiety the fact that her house was being invaded by visitors at all hours. She asserted, however, that since the apparitions she had noticed no change in the piety of her daughter, who continued to pray with the same fervor and in the same manner as in the past, just as her sisters.

In spite of the fatigue caused her by the numerous interrogations, the little visionary lent herself with the best possible grace to the inquiry of "Viscount de Montelo."

"Is it true that the Blessed Virgin appeared to you in the place called the Cova da Iria?"

"Yes, that's true."

"How many times has she already appeared?"

"Five times; once a month."

"On what day of the month?"

"Always on the thirteenth, except in the month of August when I was stopped and was led to the village to the house of the administrator. That month I saw her several days later, at Valinhos."

"They say that the Virgin appeared to you also last year, is that true?"

"It isn't true; neither last year, nor this year before the month of May. I never said that, because it isn't true."

"From where does she come? From the direction of the east?"

"I don't know. I don't see her come from any place.* When she goes away she goes toward heaven in the direction of the sunrise."

"How long does she stay? A short or long time?"

---

* This is how Lucy explains the apparent contradiction with the declaration of Jacinta. She says that "lightning" preceded the arrival of the Lady, and states that: "It wasn't really lightning, but the reflection of a light which approached little by little. In this light we could see our Lady only when she was above the evergreen oak. We couldn't explain the fact to ourselves, and to avoid questioning was the reason that we sometimes said that we saw the Lady coming, and sometimes not. When we said that we saw her coming we were speaking of this light that we saw approaching, which was *afterward* the Lady herself, and when we said we hadn't seen it come, we meant that we saw the Blessed Virgin only when she was over the evergreen oak."

"A short time."

"About the time it would take to recite a *Pater* and an *Ave,* or longer?"

"Oh, longer, much longer. But she doesn't always remain the same time; never as long as it would take to recite the beads."

"The first time you saw her, weren't you afraid?"

"Yes, and I wanted to run away with Jacinta and Francis; but she told us not to be afraid, because she didn't want to do us any harm.*

"How was she dressed?"

"She wore a white dress that reached almost down to her feet, and over it a veil of the same color, and as long as the dress. It also covered her head."

"Were there trimmings on the dress?"

"One could see on the front two gold cords which parted at the neck and were reunited at the waist by a knot also of gold."

"Did she wear a sash or a ribbon?"

"Neither of the two."

"Did she have earrings?"

"Yes, two little rings."**

"In which hand did she hold the rosary?"

"In her right hand."

"Was there a cross at the end of it?"

"Yes, a white cross."

"Did you ask the Lady who she was?"

"Yes, but she replied that she would tell me on the thirteenth of October."

"And did you ask her further, whence she came?"

"Yes, and she said, 'From heaven.' "

"When did you ask her that?"

"The second time, on the thirteenth of June."

"Did she sometimes smile, or was she sad?"

"I never saw her smiling nor sad, but always serious."

---

* Sister Lucy here adds a little commentary. "The fear which we experienced did not properly have to do with the Blessed Virgin, but rather the tempest which we believed imminent, and which we wished to flee. The apparition of our Lady inspired neither fear nor dread, but only surprise."

** Sister Lucy thus states her remembrances: "In reality I have never seen the pendants. I remember that the gold fillet, resembling a bright sunbeam, which appeared to touch the mantle, glittered in the empty space where the mantle fell from the head over the shoulders, forming undulations of light so beautiful and so varied that sometimes it made me think of little pendants. It was of that I was thinking when I gave this answer."

"Did she counsel you to recite some prayer?"

"She enjoined us to say the rosary in honor of the Blessed Virgin, for the peace of the world."

"Did she manifest a desire to see more people present, at the apparitions on the thirteenth of each month?"

"She said nothing about that."

"Is it true that she told you a secret, forbidding you to reveal it to anyone?"

"Yes, that's true."

"Did she look only at you, or did she also look at your companions?"

"She looked at all three of us."

"Could you reveal the secret at least to your confessor?"

To this question the little girl remained silent; then she appeared perplexed. I thought best not to insist.*

"They say that in order to avoid the irksome questions of the administrator, who wished to know the secret, you told him an untruth, and thus you deceived him, and then you boasted of having made fun of him. Is it true?"

"It isn't true. The administrator wished me to tell him the secret; not being permitted to do that, I refused. Without telling the secret, I told him all else that the Virgin had said to me. Perhaps that's why the administrator thought that I told the secret. But I didn't deceive him."

"Did the Blessed Virgin command you to learn to read?"

"Yes, the second time that she appeared to me."

"But if she told you that she would take you to heaven next October, of what good would it be to learn how to read?"

"It wasn't exactly that which the Lady told me; and I never thought of affirming it."

"What should be done, according to the Lady, with all the money placed at the foot of the evergreen oak at the Cova da Iria?"

"She said that it must be used to buy two little litters which would be carried, one by me, Jacinta, and two other little girls, the other by Francis and three other little boys, to the parish church. One part of the money was also to be used for the devotion and the Feast of Our Lady of the Rosary, and the rest for the construction of a new chapel."

---

* "I remained perplexed, not knowing what to reply, because I regarded as secret certain things which I was not expressly forbidden to tell. Thank God, who inspired my interrogator to pass on. I remember to have breathed a sigh of relief." (Sister Lucy.)

"Where does she wish the new chapel to be built?"

"I don't know, because she didn't say."

"Are you happy that the Virgin appeared to you?"

"Oh, yes!"

"Will she come alone on the thirteenth of October?"

"She will come with St. Joseph and the Child Jesus."

"Did she make any other revelations?"

"She told me that she would work a great miracle which would prove to everyone that she had appeared."

"For what reason do you often lower your eyes and stop looking at the Virgin?"

"Because sometimes she dazzles me."

"Did she teach you any prayer?"

"She taught me the one that we say after each mystery of the rosary."

Ourém, October 11

Two days before the date fixed by the Lady for the performing of the great wonder, Viscount de Montelo returned to Aljustrel. On the way he stopped at Vila Nova d'Ourém, with the Gonçalves family, one of the most influential of the town, from whom he obtained the following information:

"The parents of Francis and Jacinta are excellent people, deeply religious, esteemed and reverenced by all. Their father is regarded as one of the upright men of the country, incapable of telling an untruth. As regards Lucy's father, though he is not assiduous at church, he has no bad will. Her mother is a virtuous, religious, and hard-working woman."

"What do the inhabitants of Fàtima think of all that the children say?"

"First, no one believed it; but now a large number of the population place faith in the children's words. As for us, we are entirely convinced."

"On the days of the apparitions, were there extraordinary happenings? Did the people affirm having seen them?"

"The wonders are numerous and, in the month of August, almost all those who were present witnessed them. They saw a cloud descend over the evergreen oak. There was no dust on the place. However, the air seemed to be less clear than usual. The sun's light was dim. In July and August a loud clap of thunder was heard."

"Do you suspect that someone may have incited the children to put on an act?"

"No, that isn't even probable."

"Aside from the people of the country about, did many others come to see the children and talk with them?"

"Yes, an immense number, and from all directions."

"Did the children accept money if it was offered them?"

"They finally accepted some little things, but unwillingly, and only after much insistence on the part of the visitors."

"Are their families poor?"

"No, not precisely. They are in rather comfortable circumstances, and if Lucy's family hasn't more, it is her father's fault for he readily neglects the cultivation of his lands."

"What does Lucy do during the apparitions?"

"She says her rosary. If she addresses herself to the apparition, she speaks in a loud voice. I myself heard her in June, for I was near her."

"Is the place of the apparitions much frequented by the devout and the curious?"

"Yes, it is much frequented, especially on Sundays, and above all in the evening toward sunset. One sees people there from far and near; the greater number of them are not from the parish. They recite the rosary and sing well-known hymns in honor of the Virgin."

Aljustrel, the same day

After this interrogation the Viscount left for Aljustrel and went at once to the home of Lucy's parents. Her mother received him with eagerness and willingly gave him permission to question her daughter; she herself replied to a few questions which the visitor asked her.

The Mother of Lucy:

"Is your daughter related to Francis and Jacinta?"

"She is their cousin, since my husband is their mother's brother."

"How did you know that the Lady had appeared to your daughter? Was it she who told you?"

"I learned of it through the family of the other children, but Lucy had counseled her cousins to say nothing about it for fear of being scolded. After having asked her myself, she told me what she had seen."

"Did you always leave her free to go to the Cova da Iria on the thirteenth of each month?"

"I have never forbidden her to go."

"How were the children dressed when they went there?"

"The first time they were not very well dressed,* because they went in poor shepherd's clothes. On the other occasions they went to the Cova in suitable garb, and with a white veil on their heads."

"When the children were brought to the house of the administrator and kept there, did someone go to reclaim them?"

"Yes, a brother of Francis and Jacinta went to find them, but not to take them back. It was the administrator himself who brought them back home."

"Did many people come to see your daughter?"

"Yes, each day, without fail, we have visitors."

New Interrogation of Lucy:

"Listen, Lucy, you told me the other day that the money offered by the people should be carried to the parish church on two processional litters. What ought we do to procure these, and when should they be carried to the church?"

"They should be purchased with the money offered, and carried to the church on the Feast of Our Lady of the Rosary."

"Do you know exactly in what place the Virgin wishes the chapel to be erected in her honor?"

"I don't know exactly, but I think that she wants it at the Cova da Iria."

"What did she say that she would do in order that her apparition would be believed?"

"She told me that she would work a miracle."

"When did she say that?"

"Several times."

"Aren't you afraid that you will be ridiculed if nothing extraordinary happens on that day?"

"I fear nothing."

"Do you feel something in you urging you to go to the Cova da Iria on the thirteenth of each month?"

"Yes, I experience a strong desire to go there; if I couldn't do so, I would be very sad."

"Did you sometimes see the Lady make the Sign of the Cross, pray, or make the beads of the rosary glide through her fingers?"

"No, I didn't see her do any of those things."

---

* Lucy's mother seems to make a confusing statement. The first time it was on a Sunday; on those days the children went to the pasture in the clothes they wore returning from Mass.

"Did she command you to pray?"

"Yes, several times."

"Did she tell you to pray for the conversion of sinners?"

"No, she didn't say that.[*] She only told me to pray to the Virgin of the Rosary in order that the war may cease."

"Did you see what the others say that they saw — a star, or roses detach themselves from the garment of the Lady?"

"I saw no star, nor extraordinary things."

"Did you hear some noise, for instance, a clap of thunder, or a trembling of the earth?"

"Never."

"Do you know how to read?"

"No, Monsieur."

"You haven't learned how to read?"

"No."

"Is it thus that you listen to and put into practice the commands of the Lady?"

(*No reply.*)

"When you tell the crowd to kneel down and pray, is this at the Lady's command?"

"The Lady never commanded it; it is I who wish it."

"Do you remain on your knees all the time?"

"Sometimes I remain standing."

"When she speaks, is her voice gentle and pleasing?"

"Yes."

"How old does she appear to be?"

"About fifteen years old."

"Does the veil cover her forehead?"

"No, you can see her forehead."

"What kind of brightness surrounds her?"

"Something more beautiful and more brilliant than the light of the sun."

"Did she ever greet you with her head or her hands?"

"Never."

"Did you perhaps hear the conversations and cries of the crowd when you saw the Virgin?"

"No, I heard nothing."

Again, Little Jacinta:

The Viscount de Montelo next questioned Jacinta:

---

[*] In reality, says Sister Lucy, "for sinners, she commanded us to make sacrifices."

"Did the Lady bid you to say the rosary?"

"Yes."

"When?"

"When she appeared the first time."

"Did she tell you the secret too, or did she confide it only to Lucy?"

"She told me it too."

"When did she tell it to you?"

"The second time, on St. Anthony's day."*

"Did the secret perhaps have to do with making you rich?"

"No."

"Then, with making you good and happy?"

"Yes, it is for the good of the three of us."

"To make you go to heaven?"

"No."

"Can you not let me know it?"

"I can't."

"Why?"

"Because the Lady told me not to tell it to anyone."

"If the people knew the secret, would it make them sad?"

"Yes."

"How did the Lady hold her hands?"

"She held them lifted up, and often with the palms toward heaven."

"Did she have a shining halo around her head?"

"Yes."

"Could you easily gaze on her face?"

"I couldn't, because it hurt my eyes."

"Did you always understand well what the Lady said?"

"The last time I couldn't understand all of it well, because of the noise made by the crowd."

A new examination of Francis brought to light no other detail.

After the Great Prodigy

Thus Lucy Relates the Apparition:

That same evening of the thirteenth of October, Viscount de Montelo again interrogated the visionaries, at the home of the parents of Francis and Jacinta:

---

* This concerned the first secret, mentioned in the second apparition; the great secret was that of July 13.

"Is it true that the Virgin appeared to you today at the Cova da Iria?" he asked Lucy.

"Yes."

"Was she dressed as she was the other times?"

"She wore the same dress."

"Is it also true that St. Joseph and the Child Jesus were there too?"

"That's true. Yes."

"Did you see any more apparitions?"

"Our Lord also appeared, blessing the people, and the Virgin showed herself under two forms."

"What do you mean by these words, 'under two forms'?"

"I mean that she appeared dressed like the Mother of Sorrows, but without the sword in her breast. Later she was dressed . . . I don't know exactly how: somewhat like the Virgin of Carmel."

"Did you see all these apparitions at the same time?"

"No, I first saw the Virgin of the Rosary, St. Joseph, and the Child Jesus, then our Lord all alone, next, the Mother of Sorrows, and finally that which looked like the Virgin of Carmel."

"Was the Child Jesus standing, or on the arm of St. Joseph?"

"On the arm of St. Joseph."

"Was He rather large?"

"No, very little."

"About how old was He?"

"About one year old."

"Did they also appear over the evergreen oak?"

"No, they appeared near the sun, after the Virgin had left the evergreen oak."

"Was our Lord standing?"

"I saw only His head and shoulders."

"How long did the apparition over the evergreen oak last? The length of time it would take to say the rosary?"

"Not so long, it seems."

"And the persons that you saw near the sun, did they remain long?"

"No, just a little while."

"Did the Lady tell you who she was?"

"She told me that she was 'Our Lady of the Rosary.'"

"Did you ask her what she wanted?"

"Yes, I asked her."

"And what did she reply?"

"She told us to correct our faults, not to offend our Lord, already too much offended, and to recite the rosary and ask pardon for our sins."

"Did she say anything else?"

"She also expressed her wish that a chapel be erected to her at the Cova da Iria."

"With what money should this chapel be erected?"

"With the money collected there, I think."

"Did she tell you anything concerning our soldiers who died in the war?"

"No, she didn't say anything."

"Did she tell you to warn the crowd to look at the sun?"

"No, she didn't tell me that."

"Does she wish the people to do penance?"

"Yes."

"Did she use the word *penance?*"

"No, she told us to *recite the rosary,* to *correct ourselves,* and to *ask pardon of our sins from our Lord,* but she never pronounced the word *penance.*"

"When did the marvel of the sun begin? After the disappearance of the Lady?"

"Yes."

"Did you see her come?"

"Yes."

"From what direction?"

"From the east."

"And the other times?"

"I didn't notice."

"Did you see her depart?"

"Yes."

"In what direction?"

"Toward the east."

"When she left, did she go backward, or turn her back to the crowd?"

"She turned her back to them."

"Did it take a long time for her to disappear?"

"No, a short time."

"Was she surrounded by rays?"

"She always appeared shining, but this time she was dazzling. From time to time I had to rub my eyes."

"Do you think that she will appear again?"

"I think that I shall never see her again. She said nothing about this."

"Do you intend to return to the Cova da Iria on the thirteenth of next month?"

"No, Monsieur."

"Will the Virgin work some other miracles? Will she not heal the sick?"

"I don't know."

"Did you not make some request of her?"

"I told her today that I had some requests to present to her. She replied that she would accept some of them, but not the others."

"Did she tell you when?"

"No."

"Under what title does she wish that the chapel be constructed at the Cova da Iria?"

"She said today that she is *Our Lady of the Rosary.*"

"Does she perhaps wish that many people come here from all over?"

"She gave me no command concerning this."

"Did you see the signs in the sun?"

"Yes, I saw it turn around."

"Did you see any other wonderful things near the evergreen oak?"

"No, I didn't see anything else."

"When did the Lady appear most beautiful, today or the other times?"

"I have always seen her equally beautiful."

"What color was her dress when she appeared near the sun?"

"Her veil was blue and her dress was white."

"And those of our Lord, St. Joseph, and the Child Jesus?"

"They wore a red garment."

"When did you ask the Virgin what she would do in order that people would believe in her apparition?"

"The first time, in the month of June, I think; moreover, I asked her several times."

"When did she tell you the secret?"

"The second time, I think."

What Jacinta and Francis Saw:

All of this information furnished by Lucy has been confirmed by the answers of little Jacinta. As in the other apparitions so here also these two alone had heard the Lady's words. Francis was only a spectator, and often was forced to close his eyes. Here are some of their answers, made on the same day, the thirteenth of October, and then confirmed on the nineteenth.

Explanations Given by Jacinta:

"Besides the Virgin, whom did you see today at the Cova da Iria?"

"I saw St. Joseph and the Child Jesus."

"Where did you see them?"

"Near the sun."

"Did you also see near the sun, our Lord, the Mother of Sorrows, and the Virgin of Carmel?"

"No."

"But you told me on the eleventh that they would appear."

"Yes, Lucy saw the other Virgin, but I did not see her."

"Was the Child Jesus on the right or the left of St. Joseph?"

"On the right."

"Standing, or in St. Joseph's arms?"

"Standing."

"Did you see the right arm of St. Joseph?"

"No."

"How tall was the Child Jesus?"

"He didn't reach St. Joseph's waist."

"How old did the Child appear to be?"

"He was like little Deolinda de José das Neves."*

"What did the Blessed Virgin say?"

"She said we should recite the rosary every day . . . and build a chapel in the Cova da Iria."

"Did you hear that from her own lips, or did Lucy repeat it to you?"

"I heard it from her own lips."

"From where did the Blessed Virgin come?"

"From the east."

"And in disappearing, in what direction did she go?"

"Toward the east."

"Did she withdraw facing the people?"

"No, she turned her back to them."

"Did she tell you to come back to the Cova da Iria?"

"She had already said that this would be the last time, and she repeated it again today."

---

* A little girl of the place, about two years old.

"Did the Virgin tell you anything more?"

"Today she said that *the rosary should be recited every day.*"

"And where did she say it should be recited?"

"She didn't say where."

"Did she say it should be recited in the church?"

"No, she never said that."

"Where would it please you more to say it: at your house, or at the Cova da Iria?"

"At the Cova da Iria."

"Why?"

"For no special reason."

"With what money did the Virgin say the chapel should be built?"

"She said to build a chapel, but she didn't say anything about money."

"Did you look at the sun?"

"Yes."

"And what did you see?"

"I saw the sun appear red, green, and other colors; I also saw that it was turning around."

"Did you hear Lucy tell the crowd to look at the sun?"

"Yes, I heard her. In a high voice she told them to look at the sun. It was already turning."

"Did the Virgin command her to warn the crowd?"

"The Virgin said nothing."

Explanations of Francis:

"Did you also see the Virgin this time?"

"Yes."

"What name did she call herself?"

"Our Lady of the Rosary."

"How was she dressed?"

"She was dressed in white and held a rosary in her hand."

"Did you also see St. Joseph and the Child Jesus?"

"Yes."

"Where did you see them?"

"Near the sun."

"Was the Child Jesus on St. Joseph's arm or near him?"

"Near him."

"Was He large or small?"

"He was very small."

"Was He like little Deolinda de José das Neves?"

"Exactly like her."

"How did the Virgin hold her hands?"

"She kept them folded."

"Did you see her only over the evergreen oak, or also near the sun?"

"I also saw her near the sun."

"Did the sun or the face of the Virgin shine the brighter?"

"The face of the Virgin shone more."

"Did you hear what she said?"

"I heard nothing."

"Who told you the secret? The Lady?"

"No, it was Lucy."

"Can you tell me?"

"No, I cannot."

"You don't wish to speak because you are afraid of Lucy, you fear that she will strike you, isn't that true?"

"Oh, no."

"Then, why do you not want to tell me? . . . Would it perhaps be a sin?"

"I think that it would be a sin to tell the secret."

"Is the secret for the good of your soul, of Lucy's, and of Jacinta's?"

"Yes."

"Is it also for the good of the soul of the parish priest?"

"I don't know."

"Would the people be sad if they found it out?"

"Yes."

"From what direction did the Virgin come?"

"From the east."

"Did she disappear in the same direction?"

"Yes."

"Did she withdraw facing the people?"

"No, she turned around."

"Slowly or quickly?"

"Slowly."

"Did she walk as we do?"

"She didn't walk, but she went straight on, straight on, without moving her feet."

"When did she appear the most beautiful, today or the other times?"

"I always saw her equally beautiful."

"Did you also see the marvel of the sun?"

"Yes, I saw the sun turn. One might call it a wheel of fire."

"Did this marvel happen before or after the departure of the Lady?"

"As soon as she had left the evergreen oak."

"Was it the Lady who commanded Lucy to warn the crowd to look at the sun?"

"She didn't say that, but she pointed her finger in the direction of the sun before disappearing."

"And the marvel began immediately?"

"Yes."

"What colors did you see in the sun?"

"I saw the most beautiful colors: blue, yellow, and others.

The striking agreement, in general, between the independent statements of these children, ranging in ages from seven to ten years, cannot fail to convince any reader of the fact itself of the apparitions. Slight differences, or apparent differences, in their testimony, merely serve to confirm the unquestionable honesty of the children's replies, and make certain beyond all doubt the substantial truth of the visions themselves.

The historic events of Fàtima must stand unchallenged through the ages, calling upon men for the unfailing daily recital of their beads, the correction of their faults, and the earnest petition to the Sacred Heart of Jesus for the pardon of their sins, while turning to Mary for the graces to be obtained through her Immaculate Heart — to Mary, Our Lady of the Rosary, Our Lady of Light!

COLLECTIVE PASTORAL

By the Portuguese Bishops Announcing the
Accomplishment of the "Anti-Communist Vow"

The bishops of Portugal addressed a collective letter to their
faithful, during Lent of 1937, to announce the vow they had pronounced at the Cova da Iria in the preceding month of May. Their
main purpose was to organize a great national pilgrimage of
thanksgiving if our Lady saved the country from the scourge of
war and of atheistic Communism.

At the same time, the prelates recalled to the Portuguese the
damage caused by Communism and paganism, and the necessity of
practicing apostolic work and developing Catholic Action.

Now, after two years, the episcopal vow had obtained its effect.
They therefore wrote a second collective pastoral from which we
have gathered the subjoined paragraphs, confirming and illustrating
what has been said in the chapter on "The Greater Miracle."

1. *The Vow of the Bishops in 1936*

In our collective pastoral on "Communism and the Grave Prob-
lems of the Present Hour," given in Lent of the past year, we made
public the vow which we, the entire episcopate of continental Portugal, had made, pledging ourselves to head a national pilgrimage
of solemn thanksgiving to the Most Blessed Virgin, Mother of God,
on May 13, 1938, should she obtain for Portugal, of which she
is the patroness, a victory over atheistic Communism and gain for
us the favor of lasting peace.

We here transcribe the wording in which we made this vow:

"When we, the bishops of Portugal, gathered last May at the
shrine of Our Lady of Fàtima, to make there our annual retreat,
our hearts were filled with the preoccupation and anguish caused
by the unspeakable menace of those who blasphemously denied

God and sought to destroy Christianity, the family, property, and morality.

"The Vicar of Christ, the true guardian and defender of Christ's heritage, had just recently condemned the audacious impiety of these anti-Christians and had proclaimed the peril threatening the Church and society.

"Before separating, we more than once recommended ourselves and our dioceses to the special protection of the Most Blessed Virgin, victorious over all heresies, and special protectress of Portugal. We promised her, with a solemn vow, that if she preserved Portugal from the dangers menacing her and menacing the world, we would return in two years, surrounded by the faithful whom her Son had confided to us, and make, in the name of the whole nation, an act of thanksgiving to her who so often before had saved Portugal."

2. Peace in Portugal

Now, our hearts filled with gladness and with gratitude to Our Lady of Portugal, we are about to accomplish that vow.

Since 1917, when Our Lady of Fàtima appeared in the sky of Portugal, a special blessing of God has descended upon the Portuguese land. The violent movement of religious persecution has disappeared and a new period of peaceful consciences and Christian restoration has set in.

But, referring especially to the period of two years which has elapsed since our vow, one cannot fail to recognize how the invisible hand of God has protected Portugal, removing the scourge of war and the leprosy of atheistic Communism.

We made this vow in the glare of the conflagration consuming the treasures of art, religion, and education in our own sister country. Even then the rumor was spreading, not without foundation, that in their secret gatherings of satanic hate, the enemies of God and social order were preparing events of most serious consequences for Spain and Portugal.

Scarcely two months after our vow, that awful holocaust began and still continues in Spain, a conflagration seeming to menace the whole world that is now unable to defend Christianity. But Portugal, while suffering like a brother at the sight of Spain's martyrdom, has still maintained its interior peace, and has become once more what it was in the sixteenth century, the champion of Christian civilization.

The enemies of peace did not disarm. The following September, on the day dedicated to our Lady's nativity, a revolutionary movement was started even before the capital had perceived its peril. But this was at once suppressed, and Portugal could quietly pursue its way of work and progress. Now we, whose hands are pure of all the blood shed in Portugal by the spirit of revolution, can rejoice without reserve at the victory of order, for which the Church teaches respect and without which there can be neither progress nor liberty. . . .

Peace, which the Church has so urgently requested in her liturgical prayers, and for which we had petitioned at Fàtima, was granted in an almost miraculous way.

(Here the bishops recalled the historic mission of Portugal: "Born Crusader of Christianity against the Moors" and the land "which gave new worlds to the world and to Christ." Portugal is again becoming more conscious of her mission to defend Christian civilization in our day against Communism and national totalitarianism. The bishops rejoiced that their country had rightly comprehended its historic vocation.)

3. *The Defense of Christian Civilization*

For men to declare war against atheistic Communism while themselves denying Christ is not to defend Christian civilization; it is rather to oppose to the communistic peril the equally pagan oppression of the human person.

4. *The Accomplishment of the Vow and the Prayer of the Bishops*

Therefore, today we come to announce to you officially the approaching accomplishment of our vow and to invite you to join us in acquitting ourselves of that debt of gratitude.

On the next thirteenth of May, if God permits it, we, the bishops of the Metropolis, shall be at the Cova da Iria, with all the faithful who wish to join us, to thank the Most Blessed Virgin and to pray for Portugal.

We shall go there to ask God to continue to give us peace, His peace: peace in truth, peace in justice, peace in liberty, peace in progress, peace in prosperity, peace in joy.

(The letter then explains all that we must beg of God and His holy Mother in order that this reign of peace may be perfect — namely: justice and charity in the relations between men and nations; the apostolic spirit among Christians; the extension of the reign of God over all the earth; liberty for the Church to teach and sanctify souls; light from on high for public authorities; preservation from Communism and from totalitarian nationalism; a generous Christian spirit on the part of youth, etc.)

5. *Final Recommendations*

Let us prepare ourselves from now on for that great act of next May, in the way indicated by Our Lady at Fàtima: the renewal and purification of our lives by penance and ardent, incessant prayer.

(Here the letter recalls the essential message of Our Lady of Fàtima, recommends devotion to the rosary, and recalls the institution of the *Golden Book* in which the names of families are inscribed, etc.)

May Our Lady of the Rosary of Fàtima continue to protect, not only these families, but all Portugal.

Given on the Sunday of the Resurrection of Our Lord, in the year 1938.

> (Signed) *His Em. the Card. Patriarch* (*Lisbon*),
> *The Archbishop Primate* (*Braga*),
> *The Archbishop of Evora,*
> *and the ten Bishops of Continental Portugal.*

THE MESSAGE OF THE POPE

Consecrating the Church and the World to the
Immaculate Heart of Mary
(October 31, 1942)

Osservatore Romano twice published (in Portuguese and Italian)
the entire text of the Pope's message, under a large-letter title:
"The Supreme Pastor Consecrates the Church and the Human Race
to the Immaculate Heart of Mary."

Here follows the translation:

Venerable Brothers and Beloved Sons:

"Bless the God of heaven, give glory to Him in the sight of all that
live, because he has shown his mercy unto you" (Tob. 12:6).

More than once in this year of grace, in devout pilgrimages, you
have toiled up the holy mountain of Fàtima, bearing in your hearts
the whole of faithful Portugal. And there, in that oasis embalmed
with faith and piety, you laid at the protecting Virgin's feet the filial
tribute of your delicate love, the homage of your gratitude for the
immense benefits received in these last days, and also your confident
petition that she would deign to continue her protection of your
country, here and overseas, by preserving it from the great tribula-
tion afflicting the universe.

As Father of all the faithful, We make Our own, with the entire
affection of Our soul, all the sorrows and all the joys of Our children.
We unite with you in praising and glorifying the Lord, Author of all
good, so that We may render thanks to her through whose hands the
divine munificence has conferred on you such torrents of grace.

We do this with all the more pleasure since you have combined
into one and the same thanksgiving the jubilee of Fàtima and the
twenty-fifth anniversary of Our episcopal consecration.

The Blessed Virgin Mary and the Vicar of Christ on earth, two
loyalties profoundly Portuguese, and always united in the most
faithful heart of Portugal since the day when the first reconquered

lands, seed of a future nation, were consecrated to the Mother of God as "Saint Mary's Land," and when the barely constituted kingdom was placed under the protection of St. Peter.

1. *Gratitude*

"The first and the greatest duty of man is gratitude."

Nothing is more pleasing to God than a soul grateful for grace and for benefits received; and you owe a great debt to Mary, sovereign and patroness of your homeland.

In a tragic hour of darkness and discord, the Portuguese ship had lost track of its glorious traditions, misled by anti-Christian and antinational disturbances. It was sailing on to certain shipwreck, unconscious of present perils, more unconscious of those of the future whose gravity could not be judged by human prudence.

But the mercy of heaven intervened. Light shone in the darkness; out of chaos arose order; the tempest sank into a calm, and Portugal found once more the lost thread of her beautiful traditions as a most faithful nation. Once more was she to continue her route as a crusading and missionary people — even as in the days of yore, when "in the little Portuguese house there was no lack of Christian daring" to "dilate the law of life eternal" (Camoens).

Honor to those brave souls who were the instruments of Providence for so great an enterprise; but glory, blessing, and thanksgiving above all to the sovereign virgin, Queen Mother of "Mary's Land," which she has saved a thousand times and always helps in the tragic hour.

In the present affliction — perhaps the most tragic of all — she has effected it so manifestly that Our predecessor, Pius XI, of immortal memory, in the Apostolic Letter, *Ex Officiosis Litteris*, attested "the extraordinary favors with which God has blessed your country." At that date, 1934, nothing was thought of the vow of 1936 against the Red Peril, so terribly near and so unexpectedly averted. That marvelous peace had then not yet been achieved, which now, in spite of all, Portugal continues to enjoy, and which, despite the sacrifices it entails, is less ruinous than this war of extermination devastating the world.

To all these benefits still others are now added. Portugal is bathed in an atmosphere of miracles, multiplying the physical prodigies and even more the prodigies of grace and conversion which all flourish at present in that springtide of Catholic life, and give promise of such magnificent fruitage. Today, with more reason than ever, must We recognize that the Mother of God has showered extraordinary favors upon you. You then have the evident duty of returning boundless thanks to her. And certainly you have truly thanked her during this year. We know it well! Those official thanks must have been gratifying to heaven. But heaven was touched, too, by the sacrifices of the children, by the prayers and penances of the humble.

Your acts are registered in the books of God. The apotheosis of our Lady, in the procession from Fàtima to the capital of the empire during those never-to-be-forgotten days from the eighth to the twelfth of last April, was, perhaps, the greatest demonstration of faith in the eight centuries of your country.

The national pilgrimage of May 13 proved truly to be a day of heroic sacrifices, when despite cold and rain, and the enormous distances covered by foot, hundreds of thousands of pilgrims gathered to pray, to offer thanksgiving and reparation at Fàtima. Distinguished among them, bright with a renewing beauty, stood forth the example of the country's Catholic youth. In the vast gatherings of the Children's Eucharistic Crusade those little ones, so beloved to Jesus, could, with the filial confidence of innocence, protest to the Mother of God that they had performed all she asked of them: prayers, communions, sacrifices by the thousands. Hence, too, they could raise up their supplication, saying:

"Our Lady of Fàtima, it is now your turn to speak! Speak to your divine Son only one single word, and the world will be saved and Portugal will be wholly preserved from the scourge of war."

All these splendid manifestations of piety of which, under the zealous direction of the episcopate, all the dioceses and all the parishes were witness during this Jubilee Year, prove the gratitude of the Portuguese and their determination to pay the immense debt they owe their heavenly Mother.

2. Confidence

Gratitude for the past is an assurance of confidence for the future. God expects that we should thank Him for benefits received, not that He needs our thanks, but because these induce Him to render us greater benefits. It is therefore just to recognize that the Mother of God, in accepting your thanksgiving, will not leave her work unfinished, but will continue the patronage which she has granted you by preserving you from the gravest calamities.

But that your confidence may not be rash, it is necessary that each one of you, conscious of his own responsibility, should seek to merit the singular favor of the Virgin Mother, and even, as a grateful and loving son, should seek ever more truly to deserve her maternal affection. We must all listen to the maternal advice she gave at the marriage of Cana: "Whatsoever he shall say to you, do ye" (John 2:5). And He tells us all to do penance, *poenitentiam agite*, that we may strengthen our lives and avoid sin, the principal cause of the great chastisements God sends upon the world.

He tells us that in the midst of this materialistic and paganizing world, in which "all flesh has corrupted its way," we should be the salt which preserves and the lamp which enlightens, that we should cultivate purity with the greatest care, that we should show in our morals the holy austerity of the Gospel, that we should fearlessly and at all costs — as the Catholic youth protested at Fàtima — "live as sincerely convinced and 100 per cent Catholics." He finally asks us to spread about us, far and near, the sweet odor of Christ, and that by assiduous prayer, especially by the daily recital of the beads, and by the sacrifices with which zeal will inspire us, we should procure for sinful souls the life of grace and life eternal.

Then, you may invoke the Lord with confidence, and He will hear you; you may call on the Mother of God, and she will answer: "I am here." Then, not in vain will he watch who keeps the city, because the Lord will watch with him and will defend it. Then will the house built upon the foundations of a new order be more solid, because the Lord will have cemented it. Happy the people of whom the Lord Himself is God and whose Queen is the Mother of God! She will intercede and God will bless His people by granting them peace, the sum total of all benefits. *Dominus benedicet populum suum in pace.*

3. *Supplication*

But you are not lacking in zeal — who could be indifferent to the immense tragedy afflicting the world? You, on the contrary, while earnestly thanking our Lady and feeling the warmth of that mantle of love with which she enfolds you, cannot but feel the tragic contrast of those nations torn by the greatest calamity of history. Terrible manifestations of divine justice! Tremblingly, let us adore it! But let us not doubt divine mercy, for the Father who is in heaven will not forget us, even in the day of His wrath: *Cum iratus fueris, misericordiae recordaberis.*

Today, at the beginning of this fourth year of war, sadder than ever before because of the sinister developments of the conflict, today more than ever, let us have confidence in God, and in that Mediatrix whom one of Our predecessors, during the First World War, wished to be invoked as *Queen of Peace.* Let us invoke her often, for she alone can help us. She, whose maternal heart was moved at the ruins accumulating in your mother country, and who so wonderfully preserved it. She who, compassionating the sufferings of that immense misfortune by which the justice of God chastises the world, had already indicated prayer and penance as the way to salvation. She will not refuse us her maternal tenderness nor the efficacy of her patronage.

ACT OF CONSECRATION OF THE
HUMAN RACE TO THE IMMACULATE HEART OF MARY

Queen of the Most Holy Rosary, Refuge of the human race, Victress in all God's battles, we humbly prostrate ourselves before thy throne, confident that we shall receive mercy, grace, and bountiful assistance and protection in the present calamity, not through our own merits, but solely through the great goodness of thy maternal Heart.

To thee, to thy Immaculate Heart, We, as Common Father of the great Christian Family, as Vicar of Him to whom was given all power in heaven and on earth and from whom We received the care of all souls redeemed by His Precious Blood — to thee, to thy Immaculate Heart, in this tragic hour of human history, We confide, deliver, and consecrate, not only the holy Church, the Mystic Body of Jesus, now in such suffering and agony in so many places and sorely tried in so many ways, but also the entire world torn by fierce strife, consumed in a fire of hate, victim of its own wickedness.

May the sight of the widespread material and moral destruction, of the sorrows and anguish of countless fathers and mothers, husbands and wives, brothers and sisters, and innocent children, of the great number of lives cut down in the flower of youth, of the bodies mangled in horrible slaughter, and of the tortured and agonized souls in danger of being lost eternally, move thee to compassion.

O Mother of Mercy, obtain peace for us from God, and above all provide for us those graces which prepare, establish, and assure the peace.

Queen of Peace, pray for us and give to the world now at war the peace for which all people are longing, peace in the truth, justice, and charity of Christ. Give peace to the warring nations and to the souls of men, that in the tranquillity of order the kingdom of God may prevail.

Extend thy protection to the infidels and to all those still in the shadow of death; give them peace and grant that on them, too, may shine the sun of truth, that they may unite with us in proclaiming before the one and only Saviour of the world: "Glory to God in the highest and on earth peace to men of good will."

Give peace to the peoples separated from Us by error or by schism, and especially to the one who professes such singular devotion to thee and in whose homes an honored place was ever accorded thy venerable icon (today perhaps often kept hidden to await better days); bring them back to the one fold of Christ under the one true Shepherd.

Obtain peace and complete freedom for the holy Church of God; stay the spreading flood of modern paganism; enkindle in the faithful the love of purity, the practice of the Christian life, and an apostolic zeal, so that the servants of God may increase in merit and in numbers.

Lastly, as the Church and the entire human race were consecrated to the Sacred Heart of Jesus, so that in reposing all hope in Him, He might become for them the sign and pledge for victory and salvation: so we in like manner consecrate ourselves forever also to thee and to thy Immaculate Heart, our Mother and Queen, that thy love and patronage may hasten the triumph of the kingdom of God, and that all nations, at peace with one another and with God, may proclaim thee blessed and with thee may raise their voices to resound from pole to pole in the chant of the everlasting *Magnificat* of glory, love, and gratitude to the Heart of Jesus, where alone they can find truth, life, and peace.

         ❋   ❋   ❋

To all and each of the Portuguese, as pledge of heavenly blessings, We give with love and fatherly affection the Apostolic Benediction.

Pius XII

The Holy Father solemnly renewed this Act of Consecration to the Immaculate Heart of Mary on December 8, 1942, in the Vatican Basilica, in the presence of 40,000 faithful. This public act was the starting point for the general Consecration throughout the world of dioceses, parishes, and communities.

PRAYERS

1. *Between the Decades of the Rosary After the "Gloria Patri"*

O my Jesus, forgive us our sins, save us from the fire of hell, and bring all souls to heaven, especially those who most need Thy mercy.

2. *Ejaculatory Prayers*

My God, I love You because of the graces You have granted me.
My Jesus, I love You!
Sweet Heart of Mary, be my salvation!

3. *Formula of Offering*

O Jesus, it is for love of You, for the conversion of sinners, for the Holy Father, and in reparation for the sins committed against the Immaculate Heart of Mary!

4. *The Angel's Prayer*

My God, I believe, I adore, I hope, and I love You. I beg pardon for those who believe not, adore not, hope not, and love You not. (*Three times.*)

Most Blessed Trinity, Father, Son, and Holy Ghost, to You I offer, while adoring You, the Most Precious Body, Blood, Soul, and Divinity of our Lord Jesus Christ, present in all the tabernacles of the world, in reparation for the outrages by which He is Himself offended.

Through the infinite merits of His Sacred Heart and through the intercession of the Immaculate Heart of Mary, I beg for the conversion of sinners.

(NOTE: The children used to recite this prayer on their knees and with their foreheads touching the ground.)

NOVENA OF PRAYER TO OUR LADY OF FÀTIMA
(Approved by the Bishop of Leiria)

Preliminary Prayer

Most Blessed Virgin, who, on the hill of Fàtima, didst deign to reveal to three humble little shepherds the treasures of grace hidden in the practice of reciting your holy rosary, impress deeply in my soul esteem for this devotion so dear to you. Grant that, meditating on the mysteries of our Redemption therein recalled, we may gather its precious fruits.

Grant us, in particular, to obtain the grace (of . . .), which we implore through this novena, if it be for the greater glory of God, for your honor and for the good of our souls. Amen.

Our Father, Hail Mary, Glory be to the Father.

℣. Queen of the Most Holy Rosary.

℟. Pray for us.

1. *Prayer in Honor of the Joyful Mysteries* (first, fourth, and seventh days)

Most Holy Virgin, filled with the sweetest joy at the presence of the Word Incarnate, dwelling in your most pure bosom, nourished with your virginal milk, grant that we imitate on earth the purity which shone in your Annunciation, the charity which appeared in your Visitation, the tender love that you showed for Jesus in the swaddling clothes of the crib, and the humble obedience that shone out in the Temple of Jerusalem on the day of your Purification. May we also merit as a reward for our constant care in seeking Jesus here below, to find Him at last in the Temple of Glory, never to be separated from Him. Amen.

Five Hail Marys (or the beads).

2. *Prayer in Honor of the Sorrowful Mysteries* (second, fifth, and eighth days)

Most afflicted Virgin, true image of sorrow at the foot of the cross of your Son, who, after His agony and sweating of blood in the garden, after His cruel scourging and crowning with thorns, at last mounted Calvary to die there, crucified beneath your eyes, teach us the secret of that divine patience which joined you to the passion of Jesus and made you coredemptress of the human race, that we may learn of you the way of Calvary, Christian resignation in suffering, and love of the cross of your Son. Amen.

Five Hail Marys (or the beads).

3. *Prayer in Honor of the Glorious Mysteries* (third, sixth, and ninth days)

Most glorious Virgin Mary, more than any creature sharing in the triumphs of the Resurrection and the Ascension of Jesus Christ, inundated with the plenitude of the Holy Spirit who came upon you in the Cenacle; you who, after a life of perfect sanctity, were borne to heaven in body and in soul, and who did deserve to be crowned with the sublime diadem of Empress of Glory, grant that we too, following the mysteries of your glorious and triumphant life, may deserve to be one day numbered in the endless army of your devout servants, to give you, with all the elect, the perpetual homage of our hearts. Amen.

Five Hail Marys (or the beads).

℣. Pray for us, Virgin of the Rosary.

℟. That we may be made worthy of the promises of Christ.

Let Us Pray

Eternal Father, whose only Son, by His life, death, and resurrection, has merited for us the rewards of eternal life, grant to your children who meditate on the mysteries of the most holy rosary of the Blessed Virgin Mary, the grace to imitate the example contained in these mysteries and to receive the spiritual favors promised by them. Through the same Christ our Lord. Amen.

THE FIVE FIRST SATURDAYS OF THE MONTH OF
OUR LADY OF FÀTIMA

On May 13, 1939, the bishop of Fàtima published the following statement in the fifth edition of the *Official Manual of the Pilgrimage to Fàtima:*

"It is the Blessed Virgin herself who, in our days (through Sister Lucy of Jesus, the seer of Fàtima) deigned to teach us this devotion of the Five First Saturdays, whose object is to make reparation to the Immaculate Heart of Mary for all the offenses and outrages it receives from ungrateful men."

This devotion consists in:

1. Going to confession and Communion;

2. Saying the rosary;

3. Meditating a quarter of an hour on the mysteries of the rosary;

4. Having the intention of making reparation to the Immaculate Heart of Mary.

THE GREAT PROMISE

The Blessed Virgin said to Sister Lucy:

"Look, my daughter, my Heart is all pierced with thorns, which men drive into it every moment by their blasphemies and ingratitude.

"Do you at least seek to console me, and let men know that:

"I promise to assist at the hour of death, with the graces necessary for salvation, all those who on the first Saturday of five consecutive months will go to confession, receive Holy Communion, recite the beads, and keep me company during a quarter of an hour, meditating on the fifteen mysteries of the rosary, with the purpose of making reparation."

NOTE: Confession may be made eight days before or after that Communion, provided Communion is received in the state of grace. Meditation may bear on one or several mysteries of the rosary. It seems possible to meditate thoroughly on one mystery each month, so that, by making this devotion three times [i.e., for fifteen first Saturdays] all of the mysteries will have been considered.

Pious souls and religious will have a great facility in making these first Saturdays: for them, it will be sufficient, on that day, to offer their habitual rosary, for the intention indicated, and to take one or two mysteries of the rosary as their subject of meditation.

On June 13, 1912, the Holy Office had already granted a plenary indulgence, under the usual conditions, to those who will accomplish, on the first Saturday of any month, the special exercises of devotion in honor of the Immaculate Virgin Mary, in reparation for the blasphemies of which her name and prerogatives are the object. (See No. 335 of the official record: *Preces et Pia Opera*, 1938.)

Mary's request of Sister Lucy only approves and sanctions a devotion already existing and encouraged by the Church. Those who practice the devotion of the First Five Saturdays will thus fulfill the conditions required to gain the plenary indulgence granted by the Holy Office.

PRAYER TO OUR LADY OF FÀTIMA

For One's Country and for the Peace of the World

(Approved by the Archbishop of Toulouse)

O Queen of the Rosary, sweet Virgin of Fàtima, who hast deigned to appear in the land of Portugal, and hast brought peace, both interior and exterior, to that once so troubled country, we beg of thee to watch over our dear homeland and assure its moral and spiritual revival.

Bring back peace to all the nations of the world, so that all, and our own nation in particular, may be happy to call thee their Queen and the Queen of Peace. Amen.

Our Lady of the Rosary, pray for our country.

Our Lady of Fàtima, obtain for all humanity a durable peace!

ACT OF CONSECRATION TO THE
IMMACULATE HEART OF MARY*

O Immaculate Heart of Mary, Queen of Heaven and Earth, and tender Mother of men, in accordance with thy ardent wish made known at Fàtima, I consecrate to thee myself, my brethren, my country, and the whole human race.

Reign over us and teach us how to make the Heart of Jesus reign and triumph in us, and around us, as it has reigned and triumphed in thee.

Reign over us, dearest Mother, that we may be thine in prosperity and in adversity, in joy and in sorrow, in health and in sickness, in life and in death.

O most compassionate Heart of Mary, Queen of Virgins, watch over our minds and hearts and preserve them from the deluge of impurity which thou didst lament so sorrowfully at Fàtima. We want to be pure like thee. We want to atone for the many crimes committed against Jesus and thee. We want to call down upon our country and the whole world the peace of God in justice and charity.

Therefore, we now promise to imitate thy virtues by the practice of a Christian life without regard to human respect. We resolve to receive Holy Communion on the first Saturday of every month, and to offer thee five decades of the rosary each day together with our sacrifices, in the spirit of reparation and penance. Amen.

---

* This Consecration is taken from the last page of Rt. Rev. Wm. C. McGrath's *Fàtima: Hope of the World.*